From the Pages of *FATE Magazine*...

"I am delighted to be able to bring together in a single volume a selection of my cryptozoological articles that have appeared in *FATE* over the years ... so join me now on this safari of the strange and spectacular, and marvel ... at some of the fascinating zoological mysteries that have appeared exclusively in *FATE*—the world's finest and favorite magazine of the unexplained."

—*Dr. Karl P. N. Shuker*

"A must read ... In this collection of zoological 'maybes,' Dr. Karl P. N. Shuker sorts out the reality from the fiction. His encyclopedic zoological expertise has resulted in an extremely credible survey of animals which may eventually enter the accepted pantheon of animal species."

—*Roy P. Mackal, Ph.D., D.Sc.*
Professor emeritus, University of Chicago

"Dr. Shuker's knowledge of weird and wonderful creatures is truly encyclopedic, and his enthusiasm for his subject always shines out from his writing. Informative and entertaining."

—*Janet and Colin Bord*
Fortean Picture Library

"A fascinating array of mystery animals examined by a renowned zoologist and cryptozoologist. A major accomplishment!"

—*Terry O'Neill*
Editor, FATE Magazine

About the Author

An internationally recognized expert in cryptozoology (the investigation of mystery animals whose existence or identity has yet to be formally ascertained), Karl P. N. Shuker holds a Ph.D. in zoology and comparative physiology. He lives in England, where he is a freelance zoological consultant, lecturer, and writer. He has a passionate interest in cryptozoology, animal mythology, and other subjects relating to animal anomalies. During his many years of cryptozoological research, he has amassed a sizeable archive of relevant material, including books, magazine articles, newspaper reports, eyewitness accounts, and zoological specimens.

Dr. Shuker's research has taken him to many sites of cryptozoological mysteries and other unexplained phenomena, such as the Florida Everglades, the Bermuda Triangle, Moroccan snake-charming centers, Lourdes, and Loch Ness.

He is a scientific fellow of the Zoological Society of London, a fellow of the Royal Entomological Society of London, a member of the International Society of Cryptozoology, and a member of the Society of Authors.

Probably the most prolific cryptozoological writer today, he is the author of five highly acclaimed cryptozoology books, and has been a consultant and major contributor to three others. His most recent book, *The Unexplained*, is a best-selling geographical guidebook to mysteries worldwide. He has also written numerous articles for many different periodicals around the world, including *FATE Magazine*.

How to Write to the Author

If you wish to contact the author or would like more information about this book, please write to the author in care of Llewellyn Worldwide, and we will forward your request. Both the author and the publisher appreciate hearing from you and learning of your enjoyment of this book and how it has helped you. Llewellyn Worldwide cannot guarantee that every letter written to the author can be answered, but all will be forwarded. Please write to:

Dr. Karl P. N. Shuker
℅ Llewellyn Worldwide
P.O. Box 64383, Dept. K673-4
St. Paul, MN 55164-0383, U.S.A.

Please enclose a self-addressed, stamped envelope for reply or $1.00 to cover costs.
If outside the U.S.A., enclose international postal reply coupon.

From the Pages of *FATE Magazine*

From Flying Toads

to Snakes With Wings

Dr. Karl P. N. Shuker

1997
Llewellyn Publications
St. Paul, Minnesota 55164-0383
U.S.A.

Cover design: Tom Grewe
Cover art: Carrie Westfall
Editing and book design: Amy Rost

FIRST EDITION
First Printing, 1997

Library of Congress Cataloging-in Publication Data
Shuker, Karl
    From flying toads to snakes with wings: from the pages of Fate
magazine / Karl P. N. Shuker. — 1st ed.
         p. cm.
    Includes bibliographical references (p.   ) and index.
    ISBN 1-56718-673-4 (pbk.)
    1. Cryptozoology.   I. Title
QL88.3.S475   1997
590—dc21

                                                 97–10534
                                                  CIP

The chapters that compose this book have been previously published as articles in *FATE Magazine*. Refer to "From the Pages of *FATE Magazine*," page 201, for original publication dates and issues.

Illustration credits begin on page 203.

Llewellyn Publications
A Division of Llewellyn Worldwide, Ltd.
P.O. Box 64383
St. Paul, Minnesota 55164-0383
U.S.A.

Other Books by the Author

Mystery Cats of the World: From Blue Tigers to Exmoor Beasts
(Robert Hale: London, 1989)

Extraordinary Animals Worldwide
(Robert Hale: London, 1991)

The Lost Ark: New and Rediscovered Animals of the 20th Century
(HarperCollins: London, 1993)

Dragons: A Natural History
(Simon & Schuster: New York/Aurum Press: London, 1995)

In Search of Prehistoric Survivors: Do Giant 'Extinct' Creatures Still Exist?
(Blandford Press: London, 1995)

*The Unexplained: An Illustrated Guide to the World's
Natural and Paranormal Mysteries*
(J. G. Press: North Dighton/Carlton: London, 1996)

Dedication

With my very best wishes and most heartfelt thanks to everyone at FATE Magazine—the voice of tomorrow, today!

Contents

Foreword

Cryptozoology—the study of mystery animals—has become increasingly popular in recent years, bolstered by a growing interest in the unusual and unexplained. The study of mystery animals appeals to the rational scientist as well as the paranormal believer. Unlike some other fortean subjects, it is not much of a stretch to accept the possibility that there are undiscovered animals—indeed, a number of new life-forms are discovered every year and you will learn of some of the more interesting modern discoveries herein.

Many people call themselves "cryptozoologists," but very few have the requisite credentials. I have always felt that cryptozoology should be a specialty in the field of zoology. Karl Shuker has a doctorate in Zoology and Comparative Physiology from the University of Birmingham. His solid scientific foundation makes him one of those rare individuals who are able to delve into the unknown without losing their bearings. Whether speculating about the possible real-life origin of myths and legends or the identity of bizarre unidentifieds, Dr. Shuker is always lucid and compelling. I am always impressed by his ability to dig up material that is new to the cryptozoological community. Just when I think I have heard it all, he comes up with information about a newly discovered life form as strange as anything imaginable.

Karl Shuker is more than a scientist, however. He is also a devoted student of strange phenomena with a well-functioning sense of wonder. Thus, in these pages you will find quite an array of weird fish and fowl. Giant jellyfish and winged snakes are discussed alongside lake monsters and dragons.

For the paranormal enthusiast, the field holds the attraction of numerous creatures that are supposedly sighted but seem eternally elusive: Bigfoot, the Loch Ness Monster, living dinosaurs, and their ilk. Are these beings flesh and blood, or is there an aspect of them that eludes or transcends science? Or are they largely or purely a cultural phenomenon? While some of these better-known monsters occasionally make an appearance in these pages, Dr. Shuker particularly shines when discussing the lesser-known mystery creatures.

I must admit that I am somewhat partial to what Dr. Shuker refers to as the "ultra mystery" animals—strange creatures like the mulilo, the giant black sluglike beast of Zaire and Zambia. As you read this book, beware of such monsters! For they are herein, sprinkled between the real-life natural wonders. Colored horses and devil-birds cavort with a real-life Cerberus in Dr. Shuker's parade of cryptozoological curiosities.

With this book Karl Shuker has once again made a major contribution to cryptozoological literature without neglecting the non-specialist reader who will find the book accessible, stimulating, and entertaining.

MARK CHORVINSKY
Rockville, Maryland
December 1996

Preface

Some of the world's most spectacular animals remained wholly unknown to Western science until as recently as the twentieth century. Indeed, so many remarkable new animals have been discovered since 1900, or rediscovered after having been dismissed as extinct, that I recently devoted an entire book to these zoological arrivals and revivals—*The Lost Ark: New and Rediscovered Animals of the 20th Century* (1993).

The list of such creatures is an impressively long one, and is added to every year. Moreover, it seems very likely that there are many astonishing animals *still* to be officially unveiled in various remote (and sometimes not so remote) regions of the world—judging from the vast number of reports on file describing extraordinary creatures that do not correspond with any currently known by science to be alive today.

The documentation and investigation of such creatures has become the focus of a fledgling scientific discipline called cryptozoology—literally, the study of hidden animals—and a few have attracted widespread public attention. These include the monsters of Loch Ness and Lake Champlain, the yeti and Bigfoot, sea serpents from around

Dr. Karl P. N. Shuker

The author, with a model of a black panther—a popular identity for all-black mystery cats sighted in the U.S. and U.K.

the world, North America's elusive "big birds," and a diverse array of mystery cats.

In reality, these are merely the tip of the cryptozoological iceberg, yet they continue to be documented with almost tedious regularity. By ironic contrast, the vast majority of other mystery beasts are rarely if ever alluded to, even in books purportedly devoted to cryptozoological matters.

As a result, readers wishing to pursue these elusive creatures in print have no option but to risk drowning amid a deluge of specialized papers, travelogues, magazine articles, newspaper clippings, and a veritable flood of other disparate publications in search of information. Indeed, in all too many cases, obtaining relevant data and bibliographical material concerning most mystery animals can prove to be as difficult a task as seeking the animals themselves!

As a zoologist with a passionate, lifelong interest in all cryptozoological creatures, I have long been aware of this sorry situation, and it was the pressing need to rectify it that planted in my mind the seeds for this present book.

Ever since its inception way back in 1947, FATE Magazine has demonstrated a masterly ability for presenting its vast worldwide readership with an unrivaled scope and depth of coverage in relation to all types of mysterious and unexplained phenomena, including cryptozoological subjects. Consequently, I was thrilled and very honored when, in the 1980s, an initial selection of cryptozoological articles that I had submitted to FATE received a very positive response from its editor at the time, Jerome Clark, and were duly published. This began what has been a long and very happy relationship between *FATE* and myself ever since.

I have always preferred to investigate and write about lesser-known mystery animals, rather than being content merely to recycle and regurgitate familiar material regarding those earlier-mentioned select few examples. Throughout my articles for *FATE*, I have purposefully sought to bring to public attention an extensive range of unknown and unexpected animals that have previously languished in obscurity. Thanks to the great kindness, interest, and encouragement that my writings have always received from the editors of *FATE*, commencing with Jerome Clark and continuing successively with Donald Michael Kraig, Phyllis Galde, and Terry O'Neill, I have been able to achieve this goal to an extent far beyond my most optimistic expectations.

Now, for the very first time, I am delighted to be able to bring together in a single volume a selection of my cryptozoological articles that have appeared in the pages of *FATE* over the years. These have been updated where necessary to include the latest information on their subjects, and contain many of the illustrations originally accompanying them (including numerous rare and exceedingly eyecatching engravings from my private collection of pre-twentieth-century zoological illustrations). They are also supplemented by a comprehensive bibliography of the principal sources used in their preparation, which will be an essential aid to readers wishing to pursue any of this book's subjects in further detail.

Never before has any single book surveyed such a dramatic range of mysterious and controversial animals—cryptic beasts that may well share our planet, yet remain resolutely apart from the scientific world. Giant bears and serpentine sharks, death birds and devil-birds, thriving dodos and living dinosaurs, blue horses and golden-woolled sheep, Tibetan lake monsters and Zambian rainbow dragons, bat-winged cats and web-footed mice, river-lurking vampires, barking anacondas, monstrous jellyfishes, oceanic man-beasts, bird-eating deer, bloodsucking finches, rhinoceros whales, snakes with wings and jackals with horns, mermaids and master otters, Vietnamese holy goats and claw-footed pseudo-goats, Mexican onzas, flying toads, das-adders, dragonets—the list is almost endless.

So join me now on this safari of the strange and spectacular, and marvel once again at some of the fascinating zoological mysteries that have appeared exclusively in *FATE*, the world's finest and favorite magazine of the unexplained and the inexplicable.

One

Uncovering New and Rediscovered Animals

From Okapis to Onzas—and Beyond

A wise scientist does not take pride in how much he knows, but rather takes heed of how little he knows.

—Dr. Karl P. N. Shuker
The Lost Ark: New and Rediscovered Animals of the 20th Century

---

One of the greatest fallacies promoted by cryptozoological skeptics is that there can be no major new animals still awaiting discovery because none has been discovered throughout the twentieth century, and that it is quite ridiculous to speculate that long-extinct forms of animal might one day be rediscovered alive and well. In reality, however, this century has witnessed some of the most astonishing zoological arrivals and revivals of all time, unveiling such marvels as a short-necked giraffe, an armour-plated fish from an ancient lineage hitherto deemed extinct for more than sixty million years, the world's greatest ape and the world's largest lizard, a huge shark of grotesque appearance, and a whole world of new animals living in autonomous anonymity at the bottom of the ocean. All of these, and many more, were extensively documented in my book *The Lost Ark: New and Rediscovered Animals of the 20th Century* (1993). Now, a selection of the strangest and most spectacular of these long-overlooked animals is reviewed here, to provide hope and encouragement to cryptozoologists everywhere who seek the discoveries and rediscoveries of tomorrow.

A Short-Necked Giraffe Called the Okapi

One of the most famous of this century's new animals is the okapi. It first attracted Western attention in 1890, when referred to in a book called *In Darkest Africa*, by explorer Henry Morton Stanley (of "Doctor Livingstone, I presume" fame). The book mentioned a supposed "donkey" hunted by the Wambutti pygmies in the Ituri Forest of what is now Zaire (then the Belgian Congo).

However, the first tangible evidence for the existence of this mysterious beast, which the Wambutti called the okapi, was obtained a decade later. This was in 1900, when the then-governor of the Uganda Protectorate, Sir Harry Johnston, visited the Belgian fort at Mbeni in the Congo Free State. While there, he made inquiries about the okapi, and learned that the officers knew it well, and even made headbands and other items from its skin. As luck would have it, they had two of these bandoliers with them, made from the striped portion of one such skin, which they gave to Johnston. He in turn sent them to the Zoological Society of London, where it was found that the actual appearance of the stripes did not match those of any striped mammal known to science at that time.

Needless to say, Johnston implored the Mbeni officers to keep for him the next complete okapi skin that they obtained. In 1901 he was informed by the fort's commandant, Karl Eriksson, that they had procured for him not only a skin but also two okapi skulls. Very pleased with these, Johnston parceled them all up, and sent them to the director of London's Natural History Museum, the renowned zoologist Professor Edwin Ray Lankester, in order for him to identify conclusively this mysterious animal.

Far from being a donkey, the okapi proved to be a relatively short-necked forest giraffe, which Lankester christened *Okapia johnstoni* in honor of its diligent discoverer. Very different in appearance from its familiar long-necked relative, it sports a deep chestnut-violet coat, white face, long blue tongue, and vivid black-and-white stripes on its rump and upper limbs. From being the only species of its lineage alive today, the giraffe now had a living relative, one that had always been known to the pygmies, yet was a sensational new discovery for the Western world.

The okapi, Zaire's reclusive, forest-dwelling giraffe.

Great Apes and Giant Hogs

The okapi was not the only major surprise revealed in Africa at that time. A year later came the discovery of another important new mammal. As far back as 1860, the explorer John Speke had collected native reports of a huge, man-eating hairy ogre that inhabited the Virunga Volcano range of mountains (which compose the physical border between eastern Zaire, Rwanda, and Uganda), but science dismissed such stories as mere superstition and folktales.

In 1902, however, a Belgian army officer called Captain Oscar von Beringe actually shot two of these hairy "ogres," and sent them to Europe, where they were found to be a totally new form of gorilla, quite different from the lowland version, with a broader chest, longer, darker fur, and longer jaws with larger teeth. The mountain gorilla had finally been discovered. However, we now know that far from being a man-eating ogre, it is actually one of the shyest and most gentle of creature, as revealed via the studies of Dr. George Schaller, and those of the late Dian Fossey, whose life was the subject of the film *Gorillas in the Mist*.

Early photograph of a young mountain gorilla.

The mountain gorilla's debut was swiftly followed by that of another huge African mammal, the aptly named giant forest hog. With a total length sometimes exceeding seven feet, it is easily the world's largest species of wild pig. It is characterized by relatively long legs; a massive head with grotesque fungus-like warts beneath its eyes; and an extraordinary dent in the top of its skull, a dent so large that it can accommodate a man's fist. As far back as the seventeenth century, explorer Dr. Olfert Dapper had heard tales of a gigantic pig-like beast inhabiting the forests of Liberia, known to natives as the *couja quinta*; later, similar reports began to emerge from Kenya and the Congo region.

In 1903, the Kenyan reports attracted the interest of Lieutenant (later Captain) Richard Meinertzhagen of the British East African Rifles, stationed here at that time, and he decided to track this formidable beast down. In May 1904, while visiting the Nandi region of Kenya, near Lake Victoria, he succeeded in obtaining a skull, an incomplete skin, and also a smaller portion of skin from one of these creatures. He sent them all off to the mammal specialist Oldfield Thomas at the British Museum, who confirmed that the giant forest hog was a very distinct, new species, which he duly named *Hylochoerus meinertzhageni* ("Meinertzhagen's forest hog").

Congo Peacock: An Ornithological Detective Story

One of this century's most important birds also originates from Africa, and has a very unusual history. In 1913, Dr. James Chapin, an ornithologist from the American Museum of Natural History, was participating in a scientific expedition to Zaire's okapi-inhabiting Ituri Forest when he saw a native headdress containing a strange feather that he could not identify. He bought the headdress, and spent considerable time attempting to uncover the mysterious species from which this puzzling feather had derived, but all to no avail. Eventually, he placed the feather in his desk, and there it remained, still unidentified, until 1936.

During that year, Chapin visited the Congo Museum at Tervueren, Belgium. Here, on top of a dusty cabinet placed away from the museum's main collections, he spotted a pair of shabby, forgotten taxiderm birds. To his delight he could clearly see that the female had wing quills identical to his mystifying feather. Following this up, he found that its species inhabited the Ituri Forest, and was known locally as the *mbulu*, and by mid-1937 he had acquired several specimens of it for study. This revealed it to be a previously unknown species of peacock (which Chapin christened *Afropavo congensis*), the only one native to Africa, and very primitive in form, as it lacked the gorgeous fan-like train so characteristic of the familiar Asian peacocks.

Takahe: The Wanderer's Return

Another ornithological sensation of the twentieth century featured a rainbow-hued flightless rail from New Zealand's South Island—the takahe *Notornis mantelli*. Closely related to the familiar moorhen and coot, and especially to the purple gallinules of America and elsewhere, it was first discovered as a fossil, on North Island in 1847. In 1849 a living specimen was discovered on South Island, and between 1849 and 1898 a few more were also found here. After that, however, although a few were reported from time to time, these reports were never confirmed, and so science eventually wrote the takahe off as extinct. By 1948, fifty years had passed by without any having been captured or conclusively sighted.

Then in November 1948, a search was mounted by New Zealand physician Dr. Geoffrey Orbell, who had long been interested in the takahe and its history. He had even found a previously unknown lake, around whose

The head of a takahe.

shores the takahe was supposed to thrive, according to the native Maoris. Sure enough, the native reports were proven accurate, when on November 20 Orbell's team discovered some specimens alive and well. Since then, the lake's valley has become a strictly protected area, access to which is only granted to genuine researchers, ensuring that the takahes are not disturbed or threatened in any way.

The Living Dragons of Komodo

One of the most dramatic discoveries of the twentieth century must surely be that of a real-life dragon of sorts. In reality the world's largest species of lizard, measuring up to ten feet long, this formidable creature is a giant meat-eating monitor lizard, called the Komodo dragon *Varanus komodoensis*, after the tiny island in southeast Asia's Lesser Sundas chain of only 240 square miles in an area that constitutes its principal home.

The existence of a ferocious creature referred to locally as a land crocodile had long been claimed by Indonesian pearl fishers visiting Komodo, by criminals exiled here by the sultan of the neighboring island of Sumbawa, and even by an airman making a forced landing on Komodo. However, its existence was not formally confirmed until 1912. This was when J. K. H. van Steyn van Hensbroek, governor of Flores (another neighboring island), shot a specimen on Komodo measuring seven feet four inches long. He sent it to Major P. A. Ouwens, director of Java's Buitenzorg Botanical Gardens, for official documentation.

A much more recent reptilian discovery of note was that of Delcourt's giant gecko *Hoplodactylus delcourti*. For more than 150 years, France's Marseilles Natural History Museum has possessed a taxiderm specimen of a most unusual two-foot-long lizard, but no one realized that its species was totally unknown to science, until 1979, when it stirred the curiosity of the museum's latest herpetology curator, Alain Delcourt. He sent photos and its measurements to several lizard specialists worldwide, in the hope of uncovering its identity. In 1986, it was shown to be a giant gecko, but its origin remained unknown, because the museum has no record of where it had been collected.

Zoologists Drs. Aaron Bauer and Anthony P. Russell, however, consider that it probably came from New Zealand, as those species to which it is most closely related inhabit this country. Also, North Island's Maoris speak of a reputedly mythical lizard-like creature called the *kawekaweau* that is almost identical in appearance with it. As yet the Marseilles example is the only recorded specimen of Delcourt's giant gecko, but several persons have reported seeing large lizards in coastal regions of North Island that closely resemble it, so perhaps this species does still survive and will be rediscovered alive one day.

A pair of Komodo dragons.

Golden Hamster: From Extinct
Enigma to Popular Pet

It is interesting to note that some of today's most popular species of pets were hardly (if at all) known to science until this century. The golden hamster *Mesocricetus auratus* is a good example. It first gained scientific attention in 1839, when one was caught near Aleppo in northern Syria, and was exhibited at a meeting of the Zoological Society of London. Nothing more was heard of its species until 1879, when a few live specimens were brought back from Syria to Britain by James Skene, a diplomat who had been working in Syria. These thrived for a time, but after they and their progeny had died, the golden hamster sank into zoological obscurity.

During the late 1920s, Professor Israel Aharoni, from Jerusalem's Hebrew University, was reading some ancient Aramaic and Hebrew documents when he came upon the description of a strange animal called the Syrian mouse, which seemed very different from any species known to him, but had supposedly existed in the district that was now Aleppo. In April 1930, Aharoni visited Aleppo, and succeeded in capturing an adult female and eleven young specimens of this "Syrian mouse," which proved to be the same as the long-lost, virtually forgotten golden hamster.

The adult and three of the young specimens survived in captivity at the Hebrew University (the remainder had died or escaped) and began to multiply. To ensure the species' security, Aharoni distributed specimens to several scientific establishments around the world. Moreover, on account of its docile nature and attractive appearance, the golden hamster soon became popular as a children's pet, until eventually there were several million specimens in homes and pet shops worldwide.

But the most extraordinary aspect of this case is that until the 1970s, every single one of these millions had descended from the four that Aharoni had captured and maintained alive at the Hebrew University back in 1930. Not a single additional specimen had been discovered in the wild since then, until 1971, when twelve more were discovered and captured at Aleppo by U.S. scientist Dr. Michael Murphy.

Neon Tetra: Scooped from Amazonian Obscurity

Another very popular familiar children's pet worldwide is a small tropical freshwater fish called the neon tetra *Paracheirodon innesi*. Yet it was not known to science until this century.

While canoeing in 1936 along the Rio Putumayo, one of the Amazon's many tributaries, French animal collector A. Rabault saw some tiny but brilliantly colored fishes swimming in the water surrounding his canoe. He scooped up a handful to examine them, and realized that they were a totally unknown species. When they arrived back in America, their species' eye-catching neon-like fluorescent stripe made it such a favorite among aquarists that diligent attempts were made to breed it in captivity, which was eventually accomplished using slightly soft, acidic water at a temperature of up to 24°C in tanks containing water plants for spawning purposes. Today the neon tetra is a common sight in pet shops everywhere.

The Case of the Missing Macaw

Yet another interesting species popular in captivity is Lear's macaw *Anodorhynchus leari*, named after the famous nonsense-rhymes writer and bird artist Edward Lear, whose beautiful painting of one such bird in 1831 first brought this turquoise-plumed species to scientific attention. The most remarkable thing about its history, however, is that although several specimens have been exhibited in captivity since then, no one knew for certain where they had come from—not even their country of origin.

By the late 1970s, each had acquired such an air of mystery that some authorities wondered whether each really was a genuine species, or whether each was instead a hybrid between the glaucous macaw and the larger, very familiar hyacinth macaw. In January 1979, however, German-born Brazilian ornithologist Dr. Helmut Sick, who had been searching for wild specimens of Lear's macaw for fourteen years, proved the authorities wrong by finding an entire flock of Lear's macaws alive and well in a remote, little-explored area of northeastern Bahia in Brazil, called the Raso de Catarina. Another ornithological mystery had been solved.

Chacoan Peccary: The Fossil that Came to Life

In 1974, while studying the world's two known species of pig-like peccary in the semi-arid Gran Chaco area overlapping northern Argentina, western Paraguay, and southeastern Bolivia, Connecticut University biologist Dr. Ralph Wetzel was informed by the local people there that they knew of a third type of peccary—larger and quite different from the other two. They gave him some skulls of this mystery beast. When he studied the skulls, he found that they belonged to a species that science believed had died out at least 10,000 years ago, at the end of the Ice Ages.

Living specimens were soon discovered, and this resurrected species is today called the Chacoan peccary *Catagonus wagneri*. Ironically, it is now known that for years before its scientific discovery, its fur was being imported into North America to be used by New York furriers for trimming ladies' hats and coats.

Onza: Mexico's Legend Becomes a Reality

For more than 300 years, inhabitants of Sinaloa and Sonora in Mexico have reported the existence here of a large slender cat called the onza, distinct from both the puma and the jaguar; however, scientists traditionally discounted such reports as misidentifications of these latter species. Then on January 1, 1986, an onza was shot in the valley behind Sinaloa's Parrot Mountain by rancher Andres Rodriguez Murillo, who feared that it was about to attack him. A scientific team undertook a full examination of its body, and the zoological world is currently awaiting the results, which should finally disclose the onza's identity.

Although puma-like in coat color, it is much more graceful in build, comparing closely to a cheetah. It is worth noting that until as recently (geologically speaking) as the end of the Pleistocene epoch 10,000 years ago, North America did have a native species of cheetah, *Acinonyx trumani*.

Secrets of the Seas: Coelacanths, Megamouths, and More

With almost seventy-five percent of our world's surface covered by the oceans, it is not surprising that some of this century's greatest zoological finds have emerged from the depths of the seas.

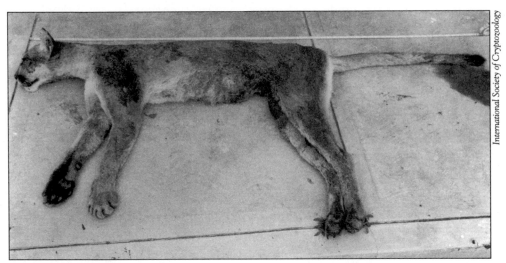

The Rodriguez onza.

In summer 1908, for example, among the many marine specimens collected by the oceanographic research ship *Albatross* was an odd crab-like creature, scooped up from the sandy bottom of the South China Sea. After being preserved and bottled, it was lodged with the vast zoological collections in Washington's Smithsonian Institution, and was afterwards largely forgotten—until 1975, that is, when it was closely examined by French scientists Drs. Jacques Forest and Michèle de Saint-Laurent. They discovered, to their amazement, that it was a modern-day member of an ancient group of crustaceans known as glyphids, hitherto believed to have died out fifty million years ago. It was formally named *Neoglyphea inopinata* ("unexpected new glyphid"), and is still the only known species of this group living today.

In December 1938, Marjorie Courtenay-Latimer, curator of the East London Museum in South Africa, visited her local docks to see if any fishes had been caught that were worth preserving as specimens for the museum. There only seemed to be a pile of sharks, but at the very bottom of the pile she noticed a strange fin sticking out. When its owner was extricated, it proved to be an extraordinary-looking fish, five feet long with thick armour-like scales, a unique three-lobed tail, and bizarre leg-like lobed fins on its body. She was unable to identify it, so she sent a drawing of it to Professor J. L. B. Smith, South Africa's leading fish specialist, who recognized to his astonishment that it was a coelacanth—a member of a prehistoric group of fishes believed to have died out more than sixty-four million years

Fortean Picture Library

The first modern-day coelacanth known to science.

ago, along with the dinosaurs. In honor of its discoverer, he named it *Latimeria chalumnae.*

No more modern-day coelacanths were found until 1952, when one was caught off the Comoro Islands near Madagascar. Since then, all of these "living fossil" fishes have been found here; no others have ever been caught in South African waters, making its headline-hitting discovery all the more remarkable and fortuitous. Ironically, although unknown to science for such a long time, the coelacanth was so familiar to the Comoro natives (who call it *kombessa*) that they often used its hard scales as sandpaper for roughening bicycle tires when mending a puncture.

In November 1976, a Hawaiian research vessel hauled up its anchor one evening only to discover an enormous shark attached to it. More than fourteen feet long, the shark had attempted to engulf the anchor in its extraordinarily large mouth, which contained more than 400 tiny teeth arranged in 236 rows. It was a dramatic, new species, one of the world's biggest sharks, yet never before recorded by science, and on account of its most outstanding feature it was christened the megamouth *Megachasma pelagios.*

Yet despite its daunting size and impressive collection of teeth, it is not dangerous. Instead, it is an inoffensive plankton consumer, spending its days in the sea depths and moving up into shallower zones during the evening, which probably explains how it has succeeded in eluding detection by humankind for so long.

Perhaps the most astonishing marine biological discovery of all time took place in 1977. An American team of scientists, led by Dr. Robert Ballard from Massachusetts's famous Woods Hole Oceanographic Institution and Oregon State University researcher Dr. John Corliss, journeyed in a U.S. Navy submarine called *Alvin* to the ocean floor near the Galapagos Islands and discovered a whole new world of animals living around sea-bottom vents there. All of the animals were new to science, never before seen by man and included enormous worms called *Riftia*, which live in eight-foot-tall tubes and sprout huge scarlet tentacles.

What was equally amazing is that this thriving community derives its energy not from the sun (sunlight cannot penetrate down through the sea to reach it) but instead from sulfur-incorporating chemical reactions occurring when gases and warm water heated by the earth's crust rise up through the vents. This community is thus a completely autonomous world, with no connection whatsoever to the rest of the planet.

Other significant aquatic discoveries from the twentieth century include eight new species of beaked whale; the Chinese river dolphin *Lipotes vexillifer*; the pa beuk or Mekong giant catfish *Pangasianodon gigas* (up to eight feet long, it is the world's largest bony fish that spends its whole life in fresh water, but remained undiscovered by science until 1930); and the Chao Phraya giant whip-tailed stingray *Himantura chaophraya* (up to fifteen and a half feet long and possibly more, it was discovered as recently as November 1987).

The Wonders of Vu Quang

If you ever meet anyone who still doubts that major new animals may yet be found, just whisper two words—"Vu Quang." This remote, little-known area of Vietnam is now one of the most cryptozoologically famous localities in the world, thanks to the unexpected discovery here of several amazing new mammals of surprisingly large size, and all as recently as the 1990s.

During a March 1992 expedition to northern Vietnam's Vu Quang Nature Reserve, headed by conservationist Dr. John MacKinnon, three skulls of an unknown antelope-like creature were obtained, bearing long dagger-like horns. The local hunters called this mysterious beast the "forest goat," but when a complete dead specimen was finally obtained it proved to be something much more spectacular. It was a radically new species of wild ox, one that, uniquely, possessed long spindly legs and extraordinary horns more akin in shape to those of the African oryxes than to any variety of ox.

**The remarkable
Vu Quang ox.**

Three young specimens have since been caught alive, but none survived for more than a few weeks in captivity. In 1993 it was christened *Pseudoryx nghetinhensis*, the Vu Quang ox, and is the largest new species of mammal to have been discovered since the Cambodian wild ox or kouprey in 1937.

But this was not the only zoological surprise that Vu Quang had in store. During March 1994, news emerged that some skulls and other remains of a giant species of muntjac or barking deer previously unknown to science had also been found here. An adult male specimen was later discovered living in a military-owned menagerie in neighboring Laos, and its species was subsequently confirmed to be new to science. The largest species of muntjac currently known, it has been appropriately dubbed *Megamuntiacus vuquangensis*.

In addition, as I pointed out in a recent article (*Wild About Animals*, March 1995), physical evidence for at least two other new species of deer has been uncovered in Vietnam.

During the 1990s, biologist Nguyen Ngoc Chinh visited a region just north of Vu Quang called Pu Mat. Here, according to local reports, a very strange deer existed, which they called the *quang khem*—"slow-running deer." Its most striking features were its antlers, for unlike the typical branched or pronged antlers of other species, those of the slow-running deer were primitive horn-like structures. Indeed, as Nguyen Ngoc Chinh could see when he finally obtained a skull from one of these animals, they closely resemble the pointed horns of a Viking's helmet. Other quang khem skulls have also been obtained, and when DNA samples from them were sent to Copenhagen University geneticist Dr. Peter Arctander for comparative analysis, he was unable to match them with those of any species of deer known to science.

But even this is not all. In a previously unstudied box of bones and other animal remains, collected in Vietnam as long ago as the late 1960s and housed since then at Hanoi's Institute of Ecology and Biological Resources, Dr. MacKinnon recently discovered an unfamiliar-looking pair of antlers. These proved to be from yet another mysterious Vietnamese deer, called the *mangden* or black deer. Neither its antlers nor its description as extracted from native testimony recalls any officially known species.

In 1994, a dramatically new species of bovine mammal was disclosed in southern Vietnam. Known locally as the *linh duong* or holy goat, it has now been formally named *Pseudonovibos spiralis*, and is characterized by ornately spiralled horns whose configuration is very like a pair of motorbike handle-bars. During 1994, zoologist Dr. Maurizio Dioli discovered that *Pseudonovibos* also exists in Cambodia, where it is called the *kting voar*.

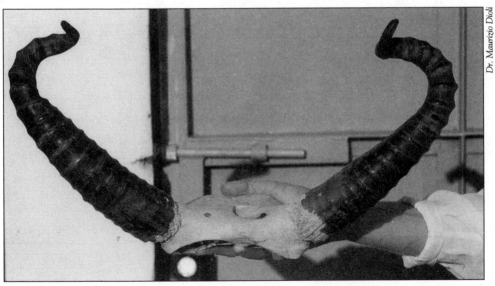

Dr. Maurizio Dioli

A pair of horns from the holy goat or *kting voar*.

While visiting Vietnam in December 1994, Doug Richardson, the London Zoo assistant curator of mammals, noticed in Hanoi's new animal market a very peculiar specimen of a lemur-related species of primate from Asia called the slow loris. It was much bigger than typical specimens, and its light cream fur was the wrong color. Yet another undiscovered species?

While the giant loris was bemusing its London observer, Dr. George Schaller from New York's Wildlife Conservation Society, was visiting Vietnam's western neighbor, Laos. Here he spied a small but strange black muntjac that could be new to science, and he was given the skull from what appears to be a specimen of the long-lost Vietnamese warty pig *Sus bucculensis*. This obscure species was first described in 1892 by a Jesuit priest but its reality has never been confirmed by any physical evidence. In addition to the skull, however, Schaller obtained a sample of meat from a recently killed specimen, indicating that it still exists.

Is there an unknown cream-furred slow loris in Vietnam?

Xenoperdix and the Bondegezou

Discovered in 1991 by Dr. Lars Dineson and some fellow zoologists from Copenhagen's Zoological Museum amid the evergreen forests of southern Tanzania's Udzungwa Mountains, but not documented by them formally until 1994 (in *Ibis*), the Udzungwa forest partridge *Xenoperdix udzungwensis* is not only a new species, but also a new genus. What makes its discovery so unexpected and exciting is that this species' closest relatives live in Asia, not Africa.

No less remarkable is the bondegezou, a very striking, sizeable new species of tree kangaroo discovered in Irian Jaya, New Guinea's western (Indonesian) half, in 1994 by zoologist Dr. Tim Flannery from the Australian Museum. Characterized by its very eye-catching black-and-white coat and its loud, whistling call, the bondegezou is well known to the local Moni and Dani tribes, but only received scientific recognition in 1995, when Dr. Flannery and two colleagues formally described it in the journal *Mammalia*.

They named it *Dendrolagus mbaiso*, which is an apt choice. *Mbaiso* is an alternative local name for the creature, translating as "the forbidden animal;" the Moni forbid their hunters to kill the bondegezou because they believe it to be their own ancestor.

The bondegezou is a major find. In the words of Dr. Flannery: "It is humbling to know that such a large and distinctive mammal as this has remained unknown to science for so long. It makes you realise how little we know about the planet we live on."

All these revelations prove beyond question that the days of incredible zoological discoveries are indeed very far from over. Tomorrow it might be the turn of Bigfoot, or the Congo's dinosaur-like *mokele-mbembe*, or one of the many forms of sea serpent to be unmasked and demystified. What will the cryptozoological skeptics say then, we wonder?

Two

Death Birds and Dragonets

In Search of Forgotten Monsters

The shaman and the scientist, even when in pursuit of the same animal, see it differently…. To a shaman a species of bat may be a blood-sucking monster; to the scientist merely a curious disease-spreading creature. That the incidence of rabies might be a quite sufficient reason for the dread in which the bat was held by the natives might not strike the scientist with such great force.

—Peter Costello
The Magic Zoo

For every well-known monster or mystery beast that has attracted worldwide interest, there is usually a varied array of equally fascinating yet virtually unknown counterparts whose histories and mysteries have been briefly recorded amid the past's morass of obscure and inaccessible literature and duly buried beneath it thereafter—until now, marking the long-overdue addition of some noteworthy yet forgotten fauna to the cryptozoological chronicles.

The Ethiopian Death Bird: An Undiscovered Vampire?

According to Slavonic mythology, the vampire is a revived corpse, little more than a gaunt zombie with long pointed teeth, which must regularly imbibe fresh blood from the bodies of the living in order to maintain its own macabre existence, eternally suspended between the animation of life and the stillness of the tomb. Surprising as it may seem, the vampire did not acquire its most famous talent, its ability to transform into a bat (demonstrated by every self-respecting Hollywood film vampire nowadays), until centuries later, after Cortes' followers returned to Europe, regaling their listeners with chilling stories of blood-drinking bats encountered during their years in Mexico. These are the *real* vampires, a trio of bat species exclusive to the Americas, which gives the following mystery beast profound significance.

Just before Ethiopia was invaded by Italian troops during World War II, archaeologist Byron de Prorok was participating in an expedition to its southern regions when he learned of a greatly feared cave near Lekempti, in the province of Walaga. Known as Devil's Cave, it was supposedly inhabited by "were-hyaenas," and, even worse, by terrible winged entities called death birds. None of the natives would willingly venture anywhere near this abode of evil, but extensive bribery procured a reluctant guide to take de Prorok there, so that he might investigate its mysteries.

Located high among rocky pinnacles and foliage, Devil's Cave was indeed frequented by hyaenas, but only of the mundane, non-transforming variety. As for the death birds, these were small bats, but de Prorok did not ascertain their specific identity. This is a great tragedy, for they allegedly exhibit a gruesome behavioral characteristic of great zoological importance.

As recounted in *Dead Men Do Tell Tales* (1943), de Prorok gained some firsthand details concerning this. When he came out of the cave after exploring it as well as he could, he was met by two of the area's goat herders, the only people frequenting this lonely, notorious locality. When he asked why everyone was so afraid of the cave's bats, they told him that these "death birds" lived on human blood, visiting their camp every night, painlessly biting them as they slept, and drinking the blood that flowed from the wounds. Eventually, the victims became so weakened by these ghoulish creatures' nightly depredations that they died, and were replaced by new goat herders.

De Prorok was skeptical, until the herders showed him their arms, which bore a number of wounds resembling small puncture marks. They also took him to their camp, and there he saw one man close to death—little more than a skeleton clothed in a shroud of ashen skin, too weak even to stand. He lay in a child's cot, and on the floor all around were blood-soaked clothes and rags.

What is so remarkable about this horrific case is that the only blood-drinking bats currently known to science are the three species of New World vampire bat. There is not a single species of sanguinivorous bat on record

Could the Ethiopian death bird be a horrific, blood-drinking bat that still eludes scientific discovery?

from the Old World! Consequently, if Ethiopia's mysterious "death birds" really are responsible for the piteous state of the goat herders living near their cave, they may constitute a known Old World species indulging in a macabre dietary deviation hitherto unrecorded, or, even more startling, an unknown species—an Old World equivalent to the neotropical vampires.

A major zoological discovery could thus await anyone intrepid enough to penetrate the grim seclusion of Devil's Cave, and pursue the dark secret of its sinister inhabitants.

Sat-Kalauk: A Burmese Bloodsucker

One of mythology's most famous bloodsucking monsters is the evil vampire cat of Japan, a feline ghoul that drains the blood of its sleeping victims at night. Less well known is that there is a real-life equivalent of sorts. This is the *sat-kalauk* or *nabashing* of Myanmar (formerly Burma), a strange cat-like beast that allegedly leaps onto the necks of sambur deer and sucks their blood.

According to the *Annual Report on Game Preservation in Burma* for the year ending March 31, 1938, one such creature, fixed firmly onto the throat of a sambur, was spied by a villager in the forests below the Maymyo Hills, but no one appeared certain of its identity.

Not long afterwards, however, the mystery was solved, following the capture of a sat-kalauk in the Indawgyi Forests of Myitkyina, northeastern Myanmar. In 1954, its species was formally identified in a *Burmese Forester* article by U Tun Yin as a yellow-throated marten *Martes flavigula*—a very large, strikingly colored relative of the European pine marten and the American fisher. Another cryptozoological creature was cryptic no more.

The Mystifying Macro of New Zealand

One of the most unlikely homes for furry mystery beasts must surely be New Zealand. Separated from all other land masses for more than sixty-four million years, this dual-island country does not harbor *any* native species of terrestrial mammal—officially. In reality, cryptozoologists have long been perplexed by the supposed existence here of a mystifying otter-like creature termed the *waitoreke*, with numerous eyewitness records on file. However, this is not the only mystery mammal documented from New Zealand.

Virtually unknown is a strange tree-climbing entity called the *macro*. In a letter of May 2, 1846, to English zoologist J. E. Gray (*Annals and Magazine of Natural History*), New Zealand's governor, Sir George Grey, noted that the natives had described to him:

> ...*another new animal which they call a "Macro;" they say it is like a man covered over with hair, but smaller and with long claws; it inhabits trees and lives on birds; they represent it as being strong and active, and state they are afraid of them. I hope in a few weeks to be able to visit the country (mountains covered with forests) which the animals live in, and as I am not afraid of them, I hope I shall send you one before long.*

Yet despite Grey's promise, nothing more was heard. As for J. E. Gray, it is clear that he was not previously aware of such a creature, because he did not mention it in his "Notes on the Materials at Present Existing Towards a Fauna of New Zealand," within Ernst Dieffenbach's *Travels in New Zealand* (1842).

There is a species of non-native mammal currently thriving in New Zealand that initially seems to provide a satisfactory identity for the macro. This is the brush-tailed possum *Trichosurus vulpecula*, a superficially lemurlike marsupial that originated from Australia. Unfortunately, the first specimens introduced into New Zealand did not arrive here until 1858.

Brush-tailed possums—not the answer to the *macro* after all.

Even the macro's name is controversial. As I learned from Canterbury Museum researcher Ron Scarlett, *macro* is a corruption. If a genuine Maori word, it would be spelled *makaro, makero, makiro,* or *makuro.* (The letter "c" does not exist in the Maori language, and consonants rarely occur consecutively within a word; they are almost always separated by a vowel.) Yet none of these, with any meaning applicable to an animal, is listed in Williams' standard *Dictionary of the Maori Language.*

Thus I concluded that if the macro is genuine, it must now be extinct, unless it never actually existed in New Zealand to begin with. Perhaps it was only a folk memory of a monkey, lemur, or Asian loris spied by the Maoris' ancestors during their travels, whose description was preserved orally through successive generations, but gradually became so distorted in the telling and retelling that it ultimately "transformed" into a seemingly unknown species allegedly frequenting the Maoris' new home, New Zealand.

This scenario is reminiscent of the version proposed by Dr. Bernard Heuvelmans in *On the Track of Unknown Animals* (1958) for Australia's bizarre *yara-ma-yha-who*—a sucker-fingered, toothless, frog-like dwarf with vampiric tendencies.

Although no such entity has ever been formally discovered here, in over-all appearance it readily recalls those small lemur-related primates from southeast Asia known as tarsiers. Accordingly, Heuvelmans suggested that perhaps the yara-ma-yha-who comprises a memory of tarsiers that was retained by Malays invading Australia prior to the white man's arrival here.

In reality, the macro is neither extinct nor a folk memory of something from beyond Australia. In fact, it never existed at all! I very recently solved the mystery of the macro while perusing through A. W. Reed's *Treasury of Maori Folklore* (1963). Once again, it contained no mention of any macro, but it did refer in detail to entities called the *maero*. Confined in most reports to South Island, the maero has been conjectured by researchers to be the last remnants of a primitive tribe of people called the Ngati-mamoe, driven by the more advanced Maoris into Fjordland's virtually inaccessible valleys and mountains.

According to traditional accounts, the maero were said to be hairy, with long fingernails that they used to catch birds and fishes. Two male maero were allegedly captured a long time ago by the Maoris of Pelorus Sound, and supposedly sported four-inch-long nails. These descriptions of the maero and Grey's report of the macro closely match one another. Their names do, too, so much so that there is little doubt that "macro" in Grey's report was simply a printing error, with "maero" as the intended name.

The maero should not be confused with a much larger, man-like entity reputedly residing on North Island's Coromandel Peninsula (and Mount Moehau in particular), east of Auckland, and variously described as silver-haired or red-furred (based respectively on sightings of old and young specimens?).

This human-sized biped is generally referred to as Coromandel Man or the Moehau Monster, and has been reported spasmodically since the late 1930s, sometimes as a single being, or as one of several inhabiting this area. Many identities have been suggested, including an undiscovered bigfoot-like species, an eccentric hermit, or a stranded extraterrestrial. More likely is that the sightings feature the last of the Morioris—a mysterious, semi-mythical pre-Maori people scarcely recorded in literature beyond the Antipodes.

Dragonets Fossilized and Formalinized

Technically, the terms *lindorm* and *lindworm* are the names given to a specific type of European dragon, one that lacks wings and only possesses a single pair of legs. However, these names are often loosely applied to small versions of the classical winged, four-legged dragon—creatures more correctly referred to as dragonets, as with the selection of examples considered here.

A surprising inclusion within the learned treatise *Mundus Subterraneus* (1678) by the Reverend Father Athanasius Kircher, a notable Jesuit scholar, was an illustration depicting a dragonet with serpentine neck and writhing tail that lived in the caverns of Switzerland's Mount Pilatus. The creature terrorized the village of Wyler until dispatched by a brave fighter called Winckelriedt. Because this region's rocks are rich in prehistoric reptile fossils, several palaeontologists have suggested that this dragonet might have been inspired by medieval fossil discoveries. In the days before scientific recognition of dinosaurs and pterosaurs, their fossils would have been labeled as dragon remains.

Winckelriedt and the baneful dragonet of Mount Pilatus.

Similarly, in 1935, R. Pusching revealed that the skull of a so-called lind-worm discovered at Klagenfurt, Austria, in 1335—which inspired the creation of a magnificent dragon-shaped fountain in the late sixteenth century and still on display today—was in reality the fossilized skull of an Ice Age woolly rhinoceros (Carinthia, II). Although based on a misidentification, the lindworm fountain can still lay claim to a certain degree of fame, for it may well be the earliest recorded attempt to reconstruct a prehistoric animal's appearance based on its fossil remains.

Equally intriguing are forgotten reports alluding to the alleged existence of preserved dragonets in various European cities and still on display as recently as the last century. For example: on December 28, 1850, in the English journal *Notes and Queries*, a semi-anonymous writer called "R. S., Jun." mentioned that:

> *When passing through the city of Brünn* [now Brno], *in Moravia* [currently part of the Czech Republic], *rather more than a year ago, my attention was drawn to the* Lindwurm *or dragon, preserved there from a very remote period…although I regret it was not in my power to examine it more particularly, evening having set in when I saw it in the arched passage leading to the town-hall of the city where it has been suspended. I fear also that any attempt to count the distinguishing bones would be fruitless, the scaly back having been covered with a too liberal supply of pitch, with the view to protection from the weather.*

This specimen had supposedly preyed upon domestic livestock and young children in the neighborhood of Brünn with impunity, until a cunning knight carefully filled the skin of a freshly killed calf with unslaked lime, and placed the corpse outside the dragonet's cave. As expected, the dragonet rushed out and consumed the offering instantly, but was then seized with an insatiable thirst incited by the lime, sending it hastening to a stream nearby, where it drank unceasingly until the water, acting upon the consumed lime, caused the hapless beast to burst!

In *Notes and Queries* for January 18, 1851, another semi-anonymous writer, "N," wrote about some other preserved "dragonets":

> *In* Murray's Handbook of Northern Italy, *mention is made, in the account of the church of St. Maria delle Grazie, near Mantua, of a stuffed lizard, crocodile, or other reptile, which is preserved suspended in the church. This is said to have been killed in the adjacent swamps, about the year 1406. It is stated to be six or seven feet long.*
>
> *Eight or ten years ago, I saw an animal of the same order and about the same size, hanging from the roof of the cathedral of Abbeville, in Picardy*

[France]. I then took it for a small croco-dile, but I cannot say positively that it was one. I am not sure whether it still remains in the cathedral. I do not know whether any legend exists respecting this specimen, or whether it owed its distinguished post to its being deemed an appropriate ornament.

The taxiderm dragons are probably specimens of crocodile or one of the large species of African or Asian monitor lizard, imported into Europe as curiosities for private ownership or as exhibits in traveling menageries. Some may have escaped and survived for a time in the European countryside, alarming anyone who unsuspectingly encountered them, until they were eventually killed. Nevertheless, if any of this chapter's readers are planning on taking a vacation in Europe, and will be visiting the cities featured in the above accounts, perhaps they could investigate whether any of these fascinating specimens are still on show, and, if they are, take some photos of them. This would greatly assist in their species' identification.

Relics purportedly from griffins—those fabulous monsters with the body of a lion but the head, wings, and forequarters of an eagle—have also been documented. Their long talons were once highly prized, because they were reputedly able to detect poison and many were brought back to Western Europe by crusaders during the Middle Ages. Sadly, however, they invariably proved to be antelope horns, sold to the gullible fighters by African entrepreneurs.

Dr. Karl P. N. Shuker

The author's cynogriffin (dog-headed griffin)—a rare beast even by cryptozoological standards.

As noted by Edward Peacock (*The Antiquary*, September 1884), a "griffin claw" preserved in the British Museum is believed to have been one of two contained in 1383 within the shrine of Saint Cuthbert at Durham Cathedral. It resembles the horn of an ibex.

The Most Horrific Hyaena Ever Known: Alive and Well in Kenya?

One of the most famous but notorious African mystery beasts is the Nandi bear of Kenya, a rapacious, bloodthirsty monster blamed for the murders of many natives and the slaughter of considerable quantities of livestock over the years. In spite of its name, however, it is almost certainly not a bear. Instead, as reasoned by Heuvelmans, it is probably a non-existent composite animal, "created" from reports describing several totally different animal types, but which have been erroneously clumped together and ascribed to a single type of mystery beast. According to Heuvelmans, its "component" creatures may include old, all-black ratels (honey badgers) *Mellivora capensis*; large (possibly unknown, giant) forms of baboon; perhaps even a surviving, claw-footed relative of the horses, known as a chalicothere; as well as some sizeable spotted hyaenas *Crocuta crocuta*, possibly of abnormal coat coloration, too.

In addition to the known existence of some abnormal spotted hyaenas, a second, much more exciting hyaena identity may also be involved here, one not previously nominated by anyone else in connection with the Nandi bear situation, yet which may render as superfluous some of the other categories noted here.

The species that I have in mind is the ferocious, short-faced hyaena *Hyaena brevirostris*. This formidable beast from the Pleistocene (two million to 10,000 years ago) was related to the smaller, present-day brown hyaena *H. brunnea*, had a very wide distribution, including Africa, and attained the dimensions of a lion. As its name suggests, its muzzle was relatively short, making its profile more bear-like than those of other hyaenas. However, the remainder of its outline was indisputably hyaenid, but on a greatly enlarged scale. It is therefore compatible with many Nandi bear reports that describe a giant hyaena-like beast with a short face and ferocious mien. Also, *H. brevirostris* seemed to have been a more active hunter than modern-day hyaenas, and thus less dependent on scavenging.

Modern-day survival of the short-faced hyaena would yield a first-class solution to many of the reports in the cryptozoologist's Nandi bear file,

Brown hyaenas—is their giant short-faced relative still alive today?

especially as this mystery creature's provenance includes forests rarely visited by Western settlers and deliberately avoided by native tribespeople—thus enabling such a species to evade scientific detection.

One particularly pertinent report, sent to me by a correspondent from Kenya, features a "giant forest hyaena" encountered by an experienced white hunter born and raised in the Nandi hills. It was shot by his father in 1962, and proved to be twice the size of a normal spotted hyaena, with long, shaggy brown hair that was very dirty on its belly. Unlike the spotted hyaena, this giant forest hyaena's body only sloped very slightly down towards its hindquarters, and its head was very large—with a skull the size of a lion's, and big, carnivorous teeth. Tragically, the carcass was not retained for formal scientific examination.

A giant hyaena-like beast is also said to inhabit parts of West Africa, including Senegal, where it is referred to as the *booaa*, after the hideous screaming cry that it emits.

Oceania's Forgotten Pygmies and Ape-Men

Among the most famous cryptozoological mysteries are North America's bigfoot, and the three distinct types of yeti reported from the Himalayas. However, there are many related versions that have received little if any widespread attention before, including several South Pacific and Australasian examples.

For instance, whereas Australia's alleged wildman or *yowie* is well known to the international cryptozoological fraternity, virtually nothing has previously emerged outside of this island continent regarding the alleged existence here of an undiscovered race of pygmies. According to one of my Australian correspondents, Bob Hay (to whom I am indebted for sending me a great deal of information concerning this subject), there is a long-standing belief in the presence of a short-statured aboriginal tribe living in Western Australia, and chance encounters with members of this elusive people have been reported from time to time.

In the mid-1970s, while driving one night along the long desolate road between Port Hedland and Broome in western Australia that he had regularly traversed for many years, a long-distance lorry driver suddenly saw a group of small, naked, dark-skinned people run across the road in front of him, clearly illuminated by his truck's powerful headlamps. Convinced that they were not simply aborigine children, he was too disturbed by what he had seen to stop and investigate. He had never seen anything like them before, and has not seen them again.

In 1956, while sitting around a campfire one evening in western Australia's Shark Bay area with several other workhands of mixed blood (i.e. of mixed aborigine and Malay background), a sixteen-year-old youth was nudged by one of his companions, who pointed to the other side of the fire. There, two workhands were communicating with a very little old man, no more than four feet tall, with dark, shriveled skin. The youth was later informed that this small, wizened being belonged to a group who periodically turned up from parts unknown in search of sugar or flour. The area's pearl fishermen of Malay extraction were reputedly terrified of these little people, refusing to spend the night alone on any part of the Shark Bay coast where they might live.

In *I, The Aboriginal* (1962), Douglas Lockwood documented the fascinating life of Waipuldanya, a full-blood aboriginal of the Alawa tribe at Roper River in the Northern Territory, who became a medical orderly, acquiring citizenship and a "white-feller" name, Phillip Roberts. According to Waipuldanya and the elders of his tribe, a race of three-foot-tall pygmies known as the Burgingin inhabits the mountains north of the Roper. They are said to be immensely strong; a Burgingin can reputedly carry a bullock on his shoulders and crush a normal man's bones. Belief in the Burgingin is not limited to the Roper vicinity either, for it extends east through the Anula and Garawa country into Queensland.

Similarly, as recently as 1994, newspapers were carrying reports emanating from Queensland's rugged Carnarvon Gorge of little hairy humanoids called the Junjuddi. Known to the aboriginals since the earliest times but often glimpsed by Westerners too, they are just over three feet tall, with ape-like limbs but a human torso, and an elongated head. Their tracks resemble those of normal children, and their cries sound like the cackling of chickens.

As documented in Brisbane's *Courier Mail* (January 29, 1994), one of their most diligent, authoritative seekers is Grahame Walsh, a former Carnarvon National Parks and Wildlife officer, who once spied fresh Junjuddi tracks near the backblocks at the headwaters of the Maranoa River. They were similar to those that a barefoot five-year-old child would make. Another race of pygmies reported from Queensland is the Dinderi, likened to small hairy people with red skin rather than brown. What could all of these pygmies be?

The most conservative explanation is that they are a type of aborigine dwarf—a mutant strain of stunted aborigines, perhaps deliberately isolated from normal aborigines as outcasts. More radically (yet perhaps more plausibly), they might constitute an ancient people whose arrival in Australia predated that of the aborigines, and who have succeeded in surviving here by keeping well away from aborigines and Westerners whenever possible.

Lending support to this theory are the enigmatic Bradshaw cave paintings discovered in the Kimberley mountains and named after the first white man to see them. Although believed by many to have been created long ago by the Kimberley aborigines, the latter people deny this, saying that these primitive works of art have been there since *before* the Dreamtime. Bob Hay has observed these curious paintings, and considers them to bear a striking resemblance to some of the cave paintings of South Africa.

Mysterious pygmies are not confined to Australia. Small, furry humanoids have been occasionally reported from New Guinea, and the Fijian islands are reputedly inhabited by a race of little people called the *vélé*. According to Constance Frederica Gordon-Cumming's *At Home in Fiji* (1882), the Kai Tholos or highlanders believe these islands' great pine forests to be frequented by "…tiny men called Vélé, with high conical heads. They carry

Was the Hawaiian wildman or *nawao* more than a myth?

small hand-clubs, which they throw at all trespassers, who go mad in consequence."

Just a folktale, or something more? A mysterious race of little people has also been reported from the Hawaiian Islands, where they are known as the *menehune*. Although these have traditionally been dismissed as mythical, in her major anthropological work *The Menehune of Polynesia* (1951) Katharine Luomala suggested that they might comprise a recent tribe of dwarfs. They had remained little-known outside of the Hawaiian archipelago until quite recently, when Fortean writer Loren Coleman documented his detailed on-site investigation of the menehune tradition (*FATE*, July 1989).

While the menehune are thus enjoying a long-overdue revival of interest, another Hawaiian "crypto-primate" remains largely forgotten. This is the *nawao*, a tall, hairy, wildman-like race. In her book *Hawaiian Mythology* (1940), Martha Beckwith chronicled the development of the early Hawaiian gods, in which the nawao are described as a race of wild people of large stature, who did not associate with man. They lived on bananas in the forest, and were numerous in earlier times, but have now disappeared.

The danger of disappearing before being formally discovered and recognized by science is the biggest threat facing mystery beasts today—not only because some of these creatures are scarce due to their retreat in the wake of more successful species, but also because of the horrific rate at which wildlife habitats are being destroyed in the name of development.

The mystery beasts of today could well become the vanished species of tomorrow, all without their erstwhile existence ever having gained official recognition. This is why, for cryptozoology, bibliographical research is just as important as fieldwork. The finding of a snippet of information concerning a hitherto unpublicized mystery beast could ultimately lead to that species' formal discovery and, with it, governmental protection, as with the okapi and other cryptozoological success stories.

Already, our modern-day world may have unknowingly lost many spectacular animals. So let us do all that we can, by carefully combing the scientific and popular literature, and by undertaking field searches, to ensure that it does not lose any more.

Three

Mystery Bears of the World

On the Trail of Ursine Unknowns

…Such a creature as no nightmare had ever brought to my imagination. I have said that he reared like a bear, and there was something bear-like—if one could conceive a bear which was ten-fold the bulk of any bear seen upon earth —in his whole pose and attitude, in his great crooked forelegs with their ivory-white claws, in his rugged skin, and in his red, gaping mouth, fringed with monstrous fangs.

—Sir Arthur Conan Doyle
"The Terror of Blue John Gap" from *Tales of Terror and Mystery*

Whereas mystery cats and, to a lesser extent, mystery dogs have attracted appreciable cryptozoological and media attention over the years, their ursine counterparts have been virtually ignored. Consequently, this is the first account to survey the surprising diversity of mystery bears on record.

Kamchatka's Irkuiem: Beware of the Bulldog Bear?

During the late 1980s, the cryptozoological grapevine was buzzing with the news that Soviet hunters with support from interested scientists were seeking a mysterious form of giant bear—as white as a polar bear but much larger in size—that apparently inhabits the region of the Russian Kamchatka peninsula bordering on the United States' Aleutian Islands.

Known to the local reindeer hunters as the *irkuiem* (sometimes spelled *irquiem*), it is said to stand four and a half feet at the withers and weigh up to one ton. It has a

Is the *irkuiem* a huge polar bear—or something even more dramatic?

small head, long limbs, and narrow body. Most intriguing of all is its curious gait, which reputedly involves putting its forelegs forward first and then pulling up its hindlimbs, likened by some to the ambulatory movements of a giant caterpillar.

Reports of the irkuiem first appeared in September 1987 in the Russian newspaper *Pravda*, followed by further Soviet reports and eventually coverage in overseas newspapers. Its most dedicated seeker is experienced hunter Rodin Sivolobov, who has collected many eyewitness accounts of the irkuiem. In 1987, he obtained from Kamchatka reindeer hunters the skin of what resembled an enormous polar bear but which the hunters adamantly insisted was from an irkueim. These giant bears are said to be rare, but are nonetheless killed occasionally.

During the winter of 1986–1987, Sivolobov had sent details of the irkuiem to noted Soviet zoologist Dr. Nikolaj Vereshchagin, who later opined that it could actually be a surviving line of the short-faced bear

Arctodus simus, believed extinct since the Pleistocene. Also called the bull-dog bear due to its unusually broad muzzle and short face, *Arctodus* was of huge stature like the irkuiem, with a squat body, long limbs, and relatively small head. An active carnivore, able to run at high speeds, it was assuredly one of the most feared predators of its time.

Vereshchagin told *Pravda* that he thought an eighth species of bear may indeed exist, and continues to await further news of the irkuiem, to discover whether it will one day be included alongside the seven spieces presently accepted by science—the brown bear, sun bear, Himalayan black bear, sloth bear, American black bear, polar bear, and spectacled bear.

It's A...A...Milne!

As it happens, however, the irkuiem is by no means unique. Indeed, there may be not only an eighth species of bear but also a ninth, tenth, eleventh, and perhaps even more species awaiting official scientific recognition, judg-ing at least from a notable dossier of reports from all over the world.

Take South America, for example. The only species of bear officially known to exist here today is the spectacled bear *Tremarctos ornatus*, a diminutive black-furred form inhabiting this continent's northwestern countries and named after the distinctive yellow-furred rings encircling its eyes. The latter markings plus its small size yield a morphology unique to this species. It cannot be mistaken for any other bear form, which therefore makes a report by explorer Leonard Clark of great cryptozoological worth.

In his book *The Rivers Ran East* (1954), Clark reported that while travel-ing with companions on a river raft, he observed an extremely large, all-black bear in northern Peru's Gran Pajonal forest. Using its powerful claws, the bear was pulling apart an ants' nest ensconced within a decaying tree stump. A noise made by the paddle of one of Clark's companions distracted this mysterious beast, which promptly dived into the river just ahead of their raft, onto which it then attempted to clamber. Clark was forced to shoot it, killing it instantly. He tried to drag its body onto the raft so that it could be preserved for formal scientific study. Unfortunately, a shoal of pira-nhas had other ideas. Clark was forced to abandon the body and to make a hasty exit.

He subsequently learned from the Campa Indians that this giant bear form was well known to them, and was referred to locally as the *milne*. He also learned that another type of mystery bear, this time red-furred, allegedly inhabited the lower eastern Andean range. Moreover, according to Dr. Bernard Heuvelmans's checklist of unknown animals (*Cryptozoology*, 1986), strange bears have also been reported from the Muscarena Mountains of Colombia. Perhaps some of the extinct bears that shared South America with the spectacled bear during the Pleistocene are not extinct after all.

Nevertheless, I do find one aspect of the milne story somewhat disquieting—its name. As I pointed out in *Secrets of the Natural World* (1993), it seems very peculiar, if not thoroughly extraordinary, that in a local South American Indian dialect, the name for this creature should be precisely the same as the surname of the creator of one of fiction's most famous bears. I am speaking, of course, of A. A. Milne, author of *Winnie the Pooh*. Just a coincidence?

Vetularctos: The Unexpected Bear

An equally mysterious, controversial bear from the New World is on record far to the north, in the Barren Ground area of Canada. On June 24, 1864, a huge yellow-furred bear was killed by two Eskimo hunters in the vicinity of Rendezvous Lake, northeast of Fort Anderson, Mackenzie. Three weeks later, Arctic explorer-naturalist Roderick MacFarlane arrived and carefully examined the dead bear's remains. Its skin and skull were preserved and ultimately reached the United States National Museum, where the creature was catalogued and thereafter largely forgotten. After all, Barren Ground had many grizzly bears, which was all this latest specimen seemed to be.

Indeed, over the next half-century the museum received many more grizzly bears, from all over North America, until such an impressive collection had been established that the renowned American naturalist Dr. C. Hart Merriam used it as he prepared a definitive review of North America's wide variety of grizzly forms. Only then did MacFarlane's mighty yellow specimen finally receive full scientific attention, as a result of which it was labeled as something very special indeed.

His detailed morphological studies suggested to Merriam that this was no ordinary Barren Ground grizzly. In fact, he felt that it was not a grizzly bear at all. Neither its hair coloration nor (of much greater taxonomic significance) its skull characteristics seemed consistent with a grizzly. In Merriam's opinion, these features were so different that he decided this anomalous bear may be more closely related to the spectacled bear and the extinct giant short-faced bear *Arctotherium* (now known as *Arctodus*, and discussed in the irkuiem section).

Consequently, he designated it as the type specimen of a totally new species—and genus—of bear, which he christened *Vetularctos inopinatus* ("the unexpected, ancient bear"), and formally documented it on February 9, 1918, in the *Survey of North American Fauna, No. 41*, produced by the U.S. Department of Agriculture's Biology Division.

Clearly, MacFarlane's unexpected, ancient bear (sometimes also called the patriarchal bear) had all the promise of being one of the twentieth century's greatest zoological revelations—a radically new species supported by incontrovertible physical evidence. Yet remarkably, it has instead slipped into almost total zoological obscurity. Nowadays, *Vetularctos inopinatus* is conspicuous only by its absence from modern publications dealing with mammalian carnivores. What went wrong?

Subsequent research into the grizzly bears of North America have suggested that the wide morphological variation leading Merriam and others to consider that many different species were present is really nothing more than individual variation. Equally, the peculiarities possessed by *Vetularctos* have been attributed by modern-day researchers to this same factor, although in the case of *Vetularctos* this explanation is not wholly convincing. The major problem is that only a single specimen of *Vetularctos* is available for study; no other is known. Added to this is the comparable dilemma (and one that is unusual for a large-sized terrestrial mystery beast) that little concerning it has been documented in the form of eyewitness accounts, local lore, or legends.

As George Goodwin noted in his own account of *Vetularctos* (*Natural History*, November 1946), the only major exception to this paucity of other evidence appears in *On Snow-Shoes to the Barren Grounds* by Casper Whitney, published toward the end of the 1800s. His book contains a passage that may well refer to *V. inopinatus*, describing a strange type of bear that, although found on the Anderson River near the Rocky Mountains, may travel as far as the Barren Ground in its search for food. Whitney wrote of:

> ...a peculiar looking bear, seeming a cross between the grizzly and the polar, and it has this peculiarity, that its hind claws are as big as the fore claws, while its head looks somewhat like that of an Eskimo dog, very broad in the forehead, with square, long muzzle, and ears set on quite like the dog's. It is very wide at the shoulders, and its robe in color resembles the grizzly.

Whitney's comparison of his strange bear to a cross between a grizzly and a polar bear is particularly interesting because several authenticated hybrids of these two species are on record. So, if Whitney's bear and MacFarlane's

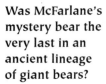

Was McFarlane's mystery bear the very last in an ancient lineage of giant bears?

Vetularctos do indeed belong to the same form, perhaps this is its true identity. Unfortunately, no one has so far attempted to pursue this possibility by comparing the remains of MacFarlane's *Vetularctos* to those of any known grizzly/polar bear crossbreed.

Some rather imprecise descriptions of giant bears are present in traditional myths of several native American tribes, as well as legends of giant polars (relevant to the irkuiem?) termed *qoqogaq* by the arctic Alaskan Eskimos, according to Diamond Jenness (*Anthropological Papers of the University of Alaska*, May 1953).

So what can we say about *Vetularctos*? Perhaps it is nothing more than an aberrant individual of the grizzly bear, or a hybrid of grizzly and polar. Alternatively, it may truly be a new species, to be verified on the procurement of further material—assuming, of course, that this bear form still exists. Yet it may do; after all, no one appears to have specifically searched for it.

Equally possible, however, as suggested by writer-naturalist Ernest Thompson Seton, is that MacFarlane's specimen was the very last survivor of a distinctive dynasty of bears whose reign climaxed in an earlier period of time. Ancient bears, known and perhaps feared by our ancestors, but ultimately reduced to a last anachronistic individual whose death in June 1864 brought the noble line of *Vetularctos* to a tragic, ignominious end.

Bergman's Giant Black Bear

Long before the irkuiem became news, the forested peninsula of Kamchatka was already noted for very large bears, though these were long-haired brown bears, first made known to science in 1898 and dubbed *Ursus arctos beringianus*. Officially, the mighty Kodiak bear *U. a. middendorffi*, with an average total length of eight feet in the male, is the largest type of bear alive today. However, in 1936, Dr. Sten Bergman noted that Kamchatka may house a gigantic, short-furred black bear form that exceeds in size all other bears.

Dr. Bergman was shown the pelt of one of these mysterious oversized beasts in the fall of 1920. He also recorded an equally colossal skull allegedly from one such bear, plus an enormous bear pawprint measuring just under fifteen inches long and ten inches wide. Both the skull and the pawprint had been observed (and, in the case of the pawprint, photographed) by fellow Swedish scientist Rene Malaise, during his nine-year inhabitation of Kamchatka.

The existence of such a bear form in this region has been supported to some extent by Russian sources, according to David Day, who noted in *The Doomsday Book of Animals* (1981) that weights of 296 pounds, 227 pounds, and 311 pounds have been recorded by Russian hunters from specimens here. However, as the most recent records concerning such huge bears as these (which have been assigned the name *U. a. piscator*) date back to the early 1920s, it must be assumed that they have since disappeared.

The Nepalese Tree Bear

Cryptozoological creatures are, by definition, animals that have succeeded in remaining hidden from scientific scrutiny. Nevertheless, in some cases specimens of such creatures have indeed been on hand (sometimes for a number of years) for scientific examination, even if scientists didn't realize it. One example involves a mysterious Nepalese bear, which may prove eventually to have been represented for several years by a living specimen in a large zoo!

Let's start at the beginning. While carrying out field work in the wooded Barun Valley around Mount Makalu's foothills in Nepal during February 1983, Drs. Daniel Taylor-Ide (director of West Virginia's Woodlands Institute) and Robert L. Fleming became intrigued by reports from local villagers that two totally different forms of bear existed in the area. One, a large, ground-living black type, was the Himalayan black bear *Ursus* (formerly *Selenarctos*) *thibetanus*, but what was the zoological identity of the smaller, more agile and arboreal type that the villagers referred to as the tree bear?

Is the Nepalese tree bear simply a young Himalayan black bear?

Eventually, some skulls of this latter bear were obtained, and it was found that their premolars and first two molars were consistently smaller than those of the Himalayan black bear. Coupling this difference with the aforementioned morphological and behavioral differences, and adding to it further details supplied by villagers, Dr. Taylor-Ide began to wonder if the tree bear could actually be a hitherto-unknown species. He proposed *Ursus nepalensis* as a scientific name for it.

But the most startling revelation was still to come. In the subsequent report prepared by J. Richard Greenwell for the *ISC Newsletter* (spring 1984) from information supplied to him by Taylor-Ide, further research had revealed that a small black bear housed for the previous two years in Kathmandu Zoo and freely observed by the zoo's many visitors may well be a living specimen of Nepal's "newly discovered" tree bear.

After securing the King of Nepal's permission, a scientific team tranquilized this enigmatic little bear and took a full set of body measurements for detailed morphometric analysis.

Further expeditions to the Barun Valley brought additional skulls to light, making a grand total of eleven. Dashing everyone's hopes, however, this new material did not provide the hoped-for proof that the team was truly dealing with a new species. Instead, as reported in a second *ISC Newsletter* report (spring 1985), it suggested the reverse. When the collection of tree bear skulls was added to others from the Himalayan black bear, a distinct transition (rather than a discrete separation) in skull size was readily apparent between the skulls from the two bear types.

This, in turn, strongly indicated that the former bear type was in reality nothing more than a juvenile version of the latter, rather than a distinct species in its own right. As for the reported differences in behavior between the two types, this could be explained as an inevitable consequence of bear overpopulation of the region. To avoid excessive competition for food and living space, the juveniles sought refuge in the trees, becoming predominantly terrestrial only when they became adults.

Although a juvenile Himalayan black bear is now the favored identity for the Nepalese tree bear, the matter has still not been conclusively resolved. Similarly, the precise range in which the tree bear phenomenon exists has yet to be defined. In a letter published by the *ISC Newsletter* (summer 1986), Raza Teshin remarked that in his book *Shikay Memoirs* (1934), Lieutenant Colonel H. S. Wood wrote that a small variety of the Himalayan black bear was readily differentiated by the Nepalese people, who call it *sano reech*.

Yet according to Teshin, Wood's favorite hunting grounds were in Assam, not in the Barun Valley area explored by Taylor-Ide and colleagues, which thereby indicates that this latter region is by no means the entire range of tree bear occurrence, whatever its taxonomic status may prove to be.

The White Bear of Shennongjia

Prior to the early 1960s, reports of all-white bears referred to as *bai-xiong* by natives of the Shennongjia mountain forests in China's Hubei Province were dismissed by scientists as confused accounts of the giant panda.

Since then, however, at least four living specimens of this creamy-colored bear have been captured and housed in zoos at Beijing and Wuhan. At first, it was assumed that these simply comprised a pale color morph (local variation) of the brown bear *Ursus arctos*, whose range of color is remarkably diverse. More recently, however, some Chinese scientists have suggested that it constitutes a separate taxonomic form, the product of a considerable period of evolution isolated from other *Ursus arctos* representatives. In short, it may be a separate subspecies—or even a distinct species—rather than a mere color form.

The Lost Atlas Bear of Africa

It is ironic that the most famous of all "mystery bears," the notorious Nandi bear of central Africa, is the one that is definitely not a bear at all, although it might well be a number of other animals (including honey badgers, hyaenas, very large baboons, and perhaps a modern-day chalicothere). Even so, Africa may possess a bona fide mystery bear too.

During the Pleistocene epoch, the Old World brown bear not only existed throughout Eurasia but also was present in much of northern Africa, represented here by the small subspecies *U. a. faidherbianus*. Such animals evidently persisted into recent times in this region, because diminutive brown bears were frequently reported here up to the Christian period, and their remains have been discovered in association with human artifacts of this date.

By the nineteenth century, however, Africa's bears had become notably rare, confined largely to Morocco's Atlas Mountains, from which the form derived its name, the Atlas bear. Although its depletion was certainly due in part to a relentless program of hunting and persecution by local inhabitants, much of the blame for its fall in numbers lay with the destruction of the vast forests that had clothed much of northern Africa in pre-Christian Roman times.

Nonetheless, as late as 1830 a specimen of the Atlas bear—a present from the Emperor of Morocco—could be seen at the Marseilles Zoological Gardens. In 1841, Edward Blyth, curator of the Royal Asiatic Society's museum at Calcutta, received the following detailed description from an Englishman called Crowther, which he duly published in the Proceedings of London's Zoological Society for that year:

> Upon questioning Mr. Crowther respecting the Bear of Mount Atlas, which has been suspected to be the Syriacus [Syrian brown bear U. a. syriacus], he knew it well, and it proves to be a very different animal. An adult female was inferior in size to the American Black Bear, but more robustly formed, the face much shorter and broader, though the muzzle was pointed, and both its toes and claws were remarkably short (for a Bear), the latter being also particularly stout. Hair black, or rather of a brownish black, and shaggy, about four or five inches long; but, on the under parts, of an orange rufous colour: the muzzle black. This individual was killed at the foot of the Tetuan mountains, about twenty-five miles from that of the Atlas. It is considered a rare species in that part, and feeds on roots, acorns, and fruits. Does not climb with facility; and is stated to be very different-looking from any other Bear.

Sadly, efforts made to preserve its skin were in vain, and it was later discarded. Even so, in 1844 this lost specimen was the basis for a formal description of the Atlas bear by Schinz, who dubbed it U. a. crowtheri, honoring its principal publicizer.

After that, reports of Atlas bears became few and far between, until by the end of the nineteenth century the Atlas bear was apparently a vanished race, at least as far as science was concerned. Moreover, its extinction marked the entire disappearance of the bear family from the African continent. Yet reports of small brown bears from these very same areas of northern Africa have continued to emerge from time to time right up to the present day.

This could be due simply to the fact that *dubb* (the Arabic name for bear) is similar in sound to *dubbah* (the name for hyaena, a species certainly present here). Yet any explanation dismissing surviving Atlas bears as illusions arising from language ambiguity must inevitably fail with those accounts that actually describe the morphology of the animals concerned. After all, small brown bears do not resemble large, striped hyaenas.

We have come a long way —right across the world, in fact—since I mentioned Dr. Vereshchagin's contemplation of the irkuiem as an eighth species of modern-day bear. The plain truth is that the irkuiem may be just the first of many such mysteries to be laid bare (or bear?) by continuing cryptozoological research.

Four

The Real "Jaws"

A Quest for Monster Sharks

One cannot look at that face without an involuntary shudder. The long flat head, and the mouth so greatly overhung by the snout, impart a most repulsive expression to the countenance; and then the teeth, those terrible serried fangs, as keen as lancets, and yet cut into fine notches like saws, lying row behind row, row behind row, six rows deep! See how the front rows start up into erect stiffness, as the creature eyes you! You shrink back from the terrific implement, no longer wondering that the stoutest limb of man should be severed in a moment by such chirurgery. But the eyes! those horrid eyes! it is the eyes that make the shark's countenance what it is—the very embodiment of Satanic malignity.

—Philip H. Gosse
The Romance of Natural History

In 1976, near the Hawaiian island of Oahu, a mighty fourteen-and-a-half-foot-long shark, accidentally hauled up from the sea, proved so radically different from all others that it required the creation of an entirely new scientific family of sharks. Its species, dubbed the megamouth *Megachasma pelagios* on account of its gigantic cavernous maw and huge rubbery lips, was a revelation. Nothing like it had ever been seen before, and its discovery provided the most potent portent since the finding of the first living coelacanth in 1938 that the oceans still conceal a great variety of major ichthyological secrets. Among these may be a number of other sharks, some of very strange form and behavior, judging from the tantalizing clues that have been documented over the years.

Sea Serpents, or Serpentine Sharks?

In August 1880, a still-unidentified creature that may well have bearing upon the subject of mystery sharks was captured at New Harbor, Maine, by Captain S. W. Hanna. According to a *Sea-Side Press* report published at that time:

> *S. W. Hanna, of Pemaquid, caught what might be called a young sea-serpent in his nets the other day. It was about 25 feet long and 10 inches in diameter in the largest part, and was shaped like an eel. The head was flat, and the upper part projected out over the mouth, which was small and contained sharp teeth. It was dead when found.*

This report attracted great interest, and U.S. Fish Commission ichthyologist Professor Spencer Baird succeeded in obtaining some more details from Captain Hanna regarding his curious catch (published in the Commission's *Bulletin* for 1883). He learned that its skin was very fine, like that of a dogfish or shark, that there was a pair of small fins placed a little way behind its head, and a single triangular fin just above them, on its back. The only other fin present was a low tail fin, similar in shape to an eel's.

Judging from a simple sketch prepared by Hanna, his fish seemed to have only three pairs of gills, uncovered like those of sharks (but all modern-day sharks possess at least five pairs, some having six or even seven). Moreover, its mouth was positioned at the very tip of its head, instead of underneath, as with all other sharks known at that time. In a letter dated September 24, 1880, Baird regarded this fish as a representative of a totally new species, but as Hanna had not preserved it, its identity is as mysterious today, more than a century later, as it was then.

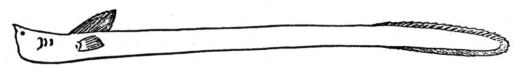

Hanna's sketch of his mysterious eel-like shark, which he drew for Professor Baird.

At the time of its capture by Hanna, its snake-like (anguinine) shape, as well as its terminally sited mouth, lent support to the view that it was a peculiar type of eel rather than any shark. The concept of a shark fashioned on this snake-like design seemed too bizarre for contemplation—until 1884.

During the years 1879 to 1881, Austrian naturalist Ludwig Döderlein brought to Vienna a collection of Japanese fishes that included two specimens of a very curious eel-like shark complete with a terminally positioned mouth, thus belonging to a species hitherto unrecorded by science. Investigations uncovered that this mysterious creature was familiar to Japanese long-line fishermen, who refer to it as the *tokagizame* ("lizard-head shark") and *ribuka* ("silk shark," describing its soft scales and fins), and capture it at depths of 600 to 1800 feet. Other Japanese specimens were obtained in the next few years, followed by some from further afield.

In 1884, Samuel Garman formally described their species, and named it *Chlamydoselachus anguineus* ("snake-like shark with frills"). Referred to in popular parlance as the frilled shark, its names allude to two of its most conspicuous features. First, its body—measuring up to six and a half feet in total length—is extremely slender, genuinely affording it an unexpectedly snake-like appearance. Secondly, the six gills on each side of its throat have frilly edges, a unique feature among modern-day sharks but exhibited by various primitive sharks dating back almost 400 million years to Devonian times. A deepwater species that preys upon octopuses and squids, the frilled shark has a wide distribution, inhabiting the Atlantic Ocean and both sides of the Pacific. Yet despite this, it is not a common species, and much of its lifestyle is unknown.

The frilled shark.

One of the most intriguing areas of speculation concerns its size. To date, the longest fully authenticated specimens do not exceed seven feet. However, if a frilled shark could attain a much greater length, its appearance would be remarkably similar to the description of a number of alleged sea serpents reported over the years. Of great interest in relation to this is the putative sea serpent washed into Sydney Harbor during August 1907 and spotted by a Rose Bay fisherman, who alerted Australian ichthyologist Dr. David G. Stead.

When Stead arrived to examine it, all that the fisherman had been able to preserve were the creature's skull and approximately 150 of its vertebrae. Nevertheless, these were enough for Stead to be able to identify it confidently as a frilled shark. Based on the number and size of the vertebrae, however, he was forced to entertain very seriously the possibility that this specimen may have been at least ten feet long in life. Its discoverer attested that it had been at least twelve feet long.

If so, this virtually doubles the officially accepted maximum length for the frilled shark, making the likelihood of even longer individuals lurking beyond the knowledge of science in the ocean's depths a lot less implausible than one might otherwise believe.

Since then, the possibility that Hanna's unidentified fish in turn belonged to some wholly unknown species of giant serpentine or eel-like shark, allied to the more diminutive frilled shark, has gained greater credence too, as expressed in Dr. Bernard Heuvelmans's *In the Wake of the Sea-Serpents* (1968). The book reiterates that the existence of such forms would satisfactorily explain certain sea serpent sightings.

Lifting the Carpet on the Ground Shark?

The frilled shark is assuredly the quintessential strange shark among all of those currently known, but it is not the only one that may well have much larger and stranger relatives still awaiting official recognition. In *The Lungfish and the Unicorn* (1941), Willy Ley mentioned that the Timor Sea, stretching between the island of Timor and Australia's northern coasts, is reputedly inhabited by a type of ferocious man-eating shark apparently unlisted by science.

According to native testimony, it is larger than the true man-eating shark (the great white shark *Carcharodon carcharias*), which also dwells in these waters and averages fourteen to fifteen feet long (rarely exceeding twenty feet). In addition, Timor's mystery shark lacks the great white's most famous trademark—its high, triangular dorsal fin. Also, in contrast to the great white's preference for swimming near the surface of the sea, the mystery shark lies in wait for its victims on the sea bottom. Stemming from such behavior, the natives term this fish the ground shark. What could it be?

As it happens, there is a very strange group of sharks whose members correspond very closely to this unidentified underwater denizen. Known as carpet sharks or wobbegongs (the Aboriginal name given to their Australian representatives but also popularly applied to their Japanese and Chinese relatives), they measure up to ten and a half feet in total length, and seem to epitomize everything that "typical" sharks are not. For whereas the latter are sleek and swift, wobbegongs are flattened and sluggish. Indeed, they look more like rays or skates than sharks at first, but the location of their gill openings on the sides of their bodies (as in other sharks) readily differentiates them (because rays and skates bear their gill openings on their undersides).

Wobbegongs owe their "carpet" appellation in part to their coloration, a much-mottled, complicated combination of browns, reds, blacks, and grays, intermingled with spots and stripes, resembling a richly patterned carpet. They also owe it to their behavior.

In stark contrast to the active hunting techniques employed by most sharks, a wobbegong prefers to await a visit from its prey (generally consisting of fishes and crustaceans). Accordingly, it spends its days reposing languorously on the bottom of shallow seas, where its flat, dappled body blends perfectly with the complex shades of its seaweed-encrusted surroundings; it becomes an invisible carpet on the sea floor. It even bears frond-like flaps of skin around its head and mouth that break up its outline

An Australian species of wobbegong.

and resemble tufts of seaweed, further enhancing its camouflage. When a potential prey victim comes within reach, however, this inanimate "carpet" abruptly comes to life and seizes the hapless creature before it has even become aware of its plight.

Although there are a few verified cases on record involving attacks by wobbegongs on divers, these unshark-like sharks are not generally viewed as being dangerous to man. But what if there were much larger wobbegongs than those known to science? Perhaps there are. After all, the unclassified ground shark's lurking, sea-bottom lifestyle is characteristic of wobbegongs; and even though wobbegongs have not just one but two dorsal fins, both are relatively small, inconspicuous structures, sited towards the rear end of the body, so they might not be readily seen by a human observer encountering a specimen beneath the water.

Could Timor's mysterious ground shark truly be an unknown, giant species of wobbegong? The concept of enormous species of shark still eluding formal detection used to be dismissed by scientists as highly improbable, but then the megamouth came along, and shark skepticism has never been the same since.

Freshwater Phantoms

Another shark in search of an identity is the unnamed inhabitant of New Guinea's Lake Sentani. Natives living in the area of this large body of freshwater (about twenty miles inland from New Guinea's northern coast) fervently believe that it houses a number of sharks. To date, all such testimony has been rejected as erroneous by science. Yet there is at least one report whose veracity is surely beyond all dispute.

During World War II, American anthropologist Dr. George Agogino was stationed at Lake Sentani, and needed to obtain some fresh fish to supply his army unit. So he dropped a hand bomb into the lake in the hope of blasting some fishes out of the water. To his astonishment, a huge creature came to the surface, one that he could readily identify as a shark, measuring at least twelve feet long. He was even able to sketch it before it sank back beneath the waters.

Although not apparently unusual in appearance, its alleged occurrence in a freshwater lake is something of a novelty, as many people believe that sharks are exclusively marine. In fact, this is not totally true. There is one species that has actually become quite famous (or, more accurately, notorious) for penetrating great distances inland via rivers and other stretches of freshwater. This singular shark is *Carcharhinus leucas*, the extremely aggressive bull shark.

So far, it has been recorded from rivers and lakes as widely dispersed as Asia's Tigris, Euphrates, and Ganges Rivers, Africa's Zambezi, South America's Amazon River, Central America's Lake Nicaragua, North America's Atchafalaya River in Louisiana and the Mississippi, assorted bodies of freshwater in Australia and the Philippines, plus, of special note, Lake Jamoer (Jamur) of northwestern New Guinea.

Needless to say, in view of the bull shark's known existence in Lake Jamoer, it would not be unreasonable to suppose that the Lake Sentani sharks are also of this species, or at least of a closely related one. So why should their very existence still be in dispute more than half a century after Dr. Agogino's sighting? Clearly this is a case in need of an intrepid ichthyologist to solve it.

Braving the Jaws of Megalodon, the Ultimate Monster Shark

The recent discovery of the megamouth, now known from nine specimens of widely separated provenances, has successfully demonstrated that even a shark as large and novel as this one can indeed exist totally undetected by science. It also encourages speculation regarding the possible survival from prehistory into the present day of one of the most terrifying sea creatures ever to have lived—a shark to end all sharks.

It has long been accepted that from twenty-five million to one million years ago (the Miocene to mid-Pleistocene times), the oceans contained a monstrous relative of the great white shark. Formally known as *Carcharodon megalodon*, and informally as the megalodon ("big tooth"), its names refer to its huge teeth, which are triangular in shape, with serrated edges, and generally measuring up to four inches long.

In 1909, their dramatic dimensions were used by scientists as the basis for early estimates of the shark's total length, yielding an immense measurement of eighty feet. The concept of a voraciously carnivorous shark little shorter than the gargantuan blue whale is horrifying in the extreme. Happily, in more recent years further studies on fossilized megalodon remains have refined this estimate considerably, reducing it to a more sedate, yet still very formidable forty-three feet.

Yet even this may not be the last word on the matter. Some extra-large megalodon teeth have been collected at the aptly named Sharktooth Hill,

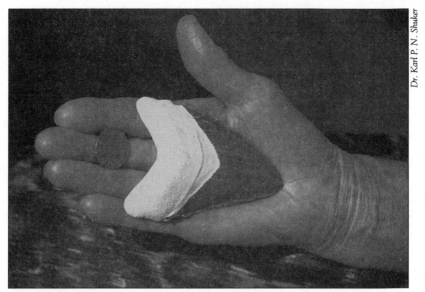

A tooth belonging to the giant megalodon shark.

near Bakersfield, California. Based on these ancient teeth—allegedly measuring almost six inches long—it is possible that some of these spectacular sharks actually attained lengths of up to fifty-five feet.

So far, the megalodon has been treated as a wholly extinct species—indisputably dynamic, but irrevocably deceased. There are tantalizing ripples running through the zoological literature, however, which intimate that the oceans may not have outlived this colossal creature after all.

In 1875, the British oceanographic survey vessel *Challenger* dredged up two megalodon teeth from a depth of over 14,000 feet, hauling them from the manganese-dioxide-rich red clay deposit on the seabed. In 1959, these were examined by Russian scientist Dr. W. Tschernezky, who investigated the thickness of the manganese dioxide layer deposited over them.

Knowing the rate of this deposition, Tschernezky was able to state that one of the teeth was not more than 24,000 years old, and the other was little more than 11,000 years old. This meant that, contrary to previous assumptions, the megalodon was still alive as recently as the end of the Pleistocene. Following on from this, is it possible that it persisted a further 11,000 years (just a brief moment in time, geologically speaking), so that this mighty species still survives today?

It is unlikely that a creature of the megalodon's forty-three to fifty-five-foot magnitude could survive undetected in modern times if it was a habitual surface-dweller. However, if it resided primarily at greater depths, only entering shallow waters infrequently, its probability of anonymity would be much greater.

Indeed, at the 1988 International Society of Cryptozoology Conference, California University shark specialist Dr. Eugenie Clark presented a paper elucidating the prospect of cryptic species of shark lurking unseen within the virtually impenetrable reaches of the oceans' stygian depths. Moreover, the megalodon's huge food requirements could be readily satisfied at such depths, because they are home to the equally spectacular giant squids, already known to be preyed upon by sperm whales. Why not by giant sharks too?

Finally, but most thought-provoking of all, my recent *In Search of Prehistoric Survivors* (1995) reveals that there are a number of compelling eyewitness accounts on record, some by experienced trawlers and other observers well versed in shark form and identity, which tell of rare encounters with

Do the oceans conceal immense meat-eating sharks that "officially" died out many millennia ago?

frighteningly large sharks resembling great whites in general shape and appearance, but which seem to have been two to three times as long. Based on fossil evidence, palaeontologists consider that the megalodon was much the same in general form and build as the great white, differing principally in absolute length. So could the sharks featured in those eyewitness accounts have been modern-day megalodons?

Perhaps the most amazing account was given by the aforementioned fish specialist Dr. David G. Stead in his *Sharks and Rays of Australian Seas* (1964). It had been narrated to him in 1918 by some fishermen at Port Stephens, New South Wales. They told him that their series of heavily weighted three-and-a-half-foot crayfish pots had been carried away once by a shark of ghostly white coloration and so extraordinarily immense that they estimated its length to have been anything between 115 and 300 feet.

Naturally, shock and surprise will distort estimations of length. However, even if we allow a very generous degree of exaggeration inspired by their sight of this awesome Moby Dick of the shark world, its length must still have been inordinately great. It seems highly unlikely that a sighting of a normal great white, which is a fairly common species in this area, would have exerted such an effect on their judgment.

In Stead's view, they had encountered a living megalodon. Added to this is his own observation of some five-inch-long teeth resembling those of great whites, which had been dredged up from the Pacific. In stark contrast to those of the megalodon currently known to palaeontologists, *these were not fossilized.*

It is a very sobering thought that the largest carnivorous shark that has ever existed might still exist, True, the megalodon may not have attained eighty feet in length. Nevertheless, even a mathematically miniaturized version reaching fifty feet or so (a full ten feet longer than the harmless whale shark *Rhincodon typus*, the world's largest known living fish) is still a creature of nightmare—effortlessly dwarfing the marauding man-made movie-star sharks to emphasize that even the most grandiose and grotesque outpourings of humanity's imagination cannot compete with the raw reality of nature.

Five

Horned Jackals & Devil-Birds

Mystery Beasts of Sri Lanka

Even in this small island [Sri Lanka], there are reports of strange animals not yet positively identified—the horned jackal, and the devil-bird with its hideous strangled shriek. Yet this jungle, even though it stretches as far as the eye can see, is nothing compared with the forests which cover much of Africa and South America. There's room for a whole zoo-full of unknown animals there. And looking at this, I am reminded of a riddle posed by an old philosopher: 'What is the most cunning of all the animals? That which no man has yet seen.'

—Arthur C. Clarke
Arthur C. Clarke's Mysterious World (TV series)

Devotees of mystery beast lore associate Sri Lanka (formerly Ceylon) with the *nittaewo*, a small forest-dwelling man-beast, but that elusive creature is by no means the only claim to cryptozoological fame of this tropical Asian island. Also awaiting formal investigation here (though largely unknown to the West) are the horned jackal and the devil-bird.

The Horned Jackal

The jackal species inhabiting Sri Lanka is *Canis aureus*, the golden jackal. In the lower country, these animals sometimes hunt in packs, and are frequently encountered on the outskirts of human settlements. Indeed, this species has gained an unsavory reputation among poultry owners, due to its taste for their livestock.

Nevertheless, both the Singhalese and Tamil inhabitants of Sri Lanka are happy to meet one member of every jackal pack: the leader. For the leader, however, that

The golden jackal, a common species in Sri Lanka.

meeting is always an unhappy occasion, since the encounter results in its death. According to a long-standing belief held by both peoples, this individual is set apart and readily distinguished from the other jackals by its possession of a small but distinctly formed horn. Generally measuring about half an inch long, this singular structure develops directly from the leader jackal's skull but is usually hidden from view by a tuft of fur.

The precise location of this horn on the jackal's skull is a little unclear. In E. Balfour's *The Cyclopaedia of India and of Eastern and Southern Asia* (third edition, 1885), the jackal horn or *narri-comboo* (also spelled *narric-comboo* or *narri-komboo*) is referred to as "a projecting process on the frontal bone [forehead] of the jackal." Yet in Sir Emerson Tennent's *Sketches of the Natural History of Ceylon* (1861), a diagram and description of a horned jackal skull show the horn as a projection from the superoccipital (posterior) region of the skull. Perhaps the horn's location varies between individuals.

In any event, the occipital position is supported by solid evidence—a preserved skull. This was the model for Tennent's diagram, and was observed by many scientists when exhibited for some years as a specimen (No. 4362 A) at London's Museum of the College of Surgeons. (See also Tennent's *Ceylon: An Account of the Island, Vol. 1*, published in 1859.)

Left: A skull of a horned jackal (arrow indicates horn); right: the horny sheath from a jackal horn.

The narri-comboo is greatly sought after by the Singhalese and Tamils, because they revere it as a powerful talisman, capable of bestowing upon its owner the realization of their every wish. It is obviously not an item to let out of one's sight, though even if it is mislaid, there should be no cause for alarm. Local lore affirms that this wonderful object has the most obliging and convenient capability of invariably returning to its careless possessor of its own accord. Another of its talents is its skill at thwarting theft; according once again to local legend, any valuable items such as jewelry will remain perfectly safe from the threat of theft as long as a narri-comboo is placed alongside them.

Most marvelous of all is the Singhalese belief that anyone possessing a narri-comboo is ever afterwards rendered invincible in any lawsuit, emerging the victor from whatever type of legal case they should find themselves involved with in the future. Tennent recounts this delightful anecdote in his aforementioned *Sketches*:

> A gentleman connected with the Supreme Court of Colombo has repeated to me a circumstance, within his own knowledge, of a plaintiff who, after numerous defeats, eventually succeeded against his opponent by the timely acquisition of this invaluable charm. Before the final hearing of the cause, the mysterious horn was duly exhibited to his friends; and the consequence was, that the adverse witnesses, appalled by the belief that no one could possibly give judgment against a person so endowed, suddenly modified their previous evidence, and secured an unforeseen victory for the happy owner of the narric-comboo!

Clearly the magic of the jackal horn is of a singularly devious nature. Moreover, it has apparently survived undiminished into modern times. As recently as 1963, for example, Harry Williams remarked in *Ceylon—Pearl of the East* (second edition) that the Singhalese consider the possession of a jackal horn to be a great prize, a charm of notable potency.

The jackal horn legend indisputably has a basis in fact. The London skull alone is proof of that. In addition, in his *Sketches* Tennent also described and figured a specimen of the horny sheath from a jackal horn presented to him by a Mr. Lavalliere, at that time the district judge of Kandy. There is certainly every chance that further specimens are preserved in Sri Lanka.

The possibility that such a horn is borne *only* by a jackal pack's leader, conversely, is much less likely. Satisfactory support for this claim is not forthcoming from either of the two plausible explanations of horn development by jackals.

One of these explanations is that horn development may be genetically induced, that is, via the action of a mutant form (allele) of some gene. Under such circumstances, however, horn production could be correlated with pack leadership only if a given leader possessed this mutant allele plus its visible expression (namely, the horn) and passed the allele on to his off-spring, which in turn became horned and also became pack leaders.

For such a contrived scenario to be at all plausible, the mutant allele would need to be dominant (to ensure its visible expression in leader off-spring) and preferably linked to the male sex (to prevent female, and hence nonleader, jackals from developing horns). Even so, this hypothesis still fails, because jackals do not always hunt in packs; some seek out prey alone or merely in pairs. Consequently, there is every chance that some jackals that inherited the horn-producing mutant allele from their pack-leader father and grew horns would not become pack leaders themselves, but would pursue an independent hunting existence instead.

In short, although it is certainly possible that horn development in jack-als is genetically induced, such an explanation cannot lend support to the native belief that such development is restricted to pack leaders.

The second plausible explanation for the jackal horn's production is that it occurs by virtue of a skin disorder (as with the induction of aberrant horns by warts) or physical violence. In *More Animal Legends* (1959), zool-ogist Dr. Maurice Burton reported that sometimes because of an injury received during a fight, a horn will grow from the center of a deer's forehead (i.e. from its frontal bones). Perhaps the jackal horn is of comparable origin. Such a mechanism could resolve the uncertainty concerning its precise location upon the skull; horn development may ensue from any cranial region receiving a severe blow.

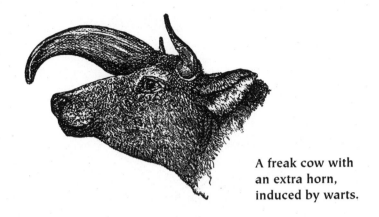

**A freak cow with
an extra horn,
induced by warts.**

At the same time, though pack leadership is inevitably accompanied by exposure to injury, nonleader pack members (as well as solitary jackals) are certainly not immune to injury either. Again, therefore, we find no support for the native belief that the jackal horn is unique to pack leaders.

References to horned dogs (not to mention horned cats, hares, horses, pigs, and other cornute curiosities) are contained within a number of medieval works. These include: Georgius Francus' *Tractatus Philologico-Medicus de Cornutis in quo varia curiosa delibantur ex Theologorum, Jctorum, Medicorum, Philosophorum, Politicorum atque Philologorum monumentis* (published in 1678); Thomas Broderus Birckerodius' *Sciagraphia…sive De Cornibus et Cornutis commentariorum quos ex omni antiquitate, scientia, & arte collectos, sex libris distinctos, figuris marmorum, statuarum, gemmarum…* (c.1694); and Christianus Franciscus Paullinus' *Lagographia Curiosa Seu Leporis Descriptio, Juxta Methodum & Leges…* (1691); plus various others with equally concise, readily recalled titles. Sadly, many accounts from these tomes are so interwoven with myth and folklore that it is virtually impossible to disentangle fact from fiction, thereby reducing their value as sources of information concerning animal anomalies.

In the case of horned dogs, however, it is evident that one genuine example still persists in Sri Lanka. Let us hope, therefore, that its horned jackals will engender serious research interest in the near future. It would be a great loss to science if such remarkable beasts should disappear, unstudied and unexplained, though it seems likely that Sri Lanka's prosecution lawyers would not weep many tears if jackal horns did vanish for good!

Devil-Birds

Whereas the horned jackal, although indisputably odd, is nothing more than an intraspecific oddity, the identity of the devil-bird is far less easily resolved. For a detailed account of this mysterious and macabre creature, let us turn again to Tennent's *Sketches*:

> *Of the nocturnal accipitres the most remarkable is the brown owl, which, from its hideous yell, has acquired the name of the "Devil-Bird." The Singhalese regard it literally with horror, and its scream by night in the vicinity of a village is bewailed as the harbinger of impending calamity. There is a popular legend in connection with it, to the effect that a morose and savage husband, who suspected the fidelity of his wife, availed himself of her absence to kill her child, of whose paternity he was doubtful, and on her return placed before her a curry prepared from its flesh. Of this the unhappy woman partook, till discovering the crime by finding the finger of her infant, she fled in frenzy to the forest, and there destroyed herself. On her death she was metamorphosed, according to the Buddhist belief, into an ulama, or Devil-bird, which still at nightfall horrifies the villagers by repeating the frantic screams of the bereaved mother in her agony.*

Many other comparable accounts are also on record. As far back as 1681, for example, Knox's *Ceylon* contained a piece that clearly refers to the same creature, although in this instance a theological rather than a zoological explanation is offered for the origin of the horrific shrieks. The item states:

> *This for certain I can affirm, That oftentimes the Devil doth cry with an audible Voice in the Night; 'tis very shrill, almost like the barking of a Dog. This I have often heard myself; but never heard that he did anybody any harm…To believe that this is the Voice of the Devil these reasons urge, because there is no Creature known to the Inhabitants, that cry like it, and because it will on a sudden depart from one place, and make a noise in another, quicker than any fowl could fly; and because the very Dogs will tremble and shake when they hear it.*

In 1849, Pridham's *Ceylon* contained the following description:

> *Devil's Bird (Strix Gaulama or Ulama, Singh). A species of owl. The wild and wailing cry of this bird is considered a sure presage of death and misfortune, unless measures be taken to avert its infernal threats, and refuse its warning. Though often heard even on the tops of their houses, the natives maintain that it has never been caught or distinctly seen, and they consider it to be one of the most annoying of the evil spirits which haunt their country.*

In 1881, Haeckel's *Visit to Ceylon* mentioned "the uncanny cry of the devil-bird, Syrnium Indrani...."

Strix gaulama, Strix ulama, and *Syrnium indrani* are all scientific synonyms of the brown wood owl, nowadays referred to as *Strix leptogrammica.* Its Sri Lankan representative is the dark subspecies *S. l. ochrogenys*—known to the Singhalese as the *ulama,* and to the Tamils as the *andai*—which occurs very widely throughout the island. Stoutly built, measuring just under twenty inches, the Sri Lankan brown wood owl is distinguished from all other owls here by its diagnostic combination of white eyebrows, eyes each encircled by a broad black ring and set in a paler facial disc, and buff-white underparts bearing narrow transverse bars of brown.

If the devil-bird is nothing more than the brown wood owl, why should this be of any interest to cryptozoologists? Surely there is no mystery awaiting a solution?

It turns out that it is by no means certain that devil-birds are brown wood owls. Indeed, this appears to be little more than an identification of convenience, which in reality contains discrepancies and raises a host of unanswered questions.

A Sri Lankan brown wood owl.

Is the devil-bird a love-struck eagle owl?

Dr. Karl P. N. Shuker

For instance, in Norah Burke's *Eleven Leopards: A Journey Through the Jungles of Ceylon* (1965), a second owl species is offered as the culprit. Burke notes that some Sri Lankans believe that the devil-bird's bloodcurdling screams are actually "the love-song of the forest eagle owl." This theory has also been put forward by George Morrison Henry in *A Guide to the Birds of Ceylon* (1955). Sri Lanka's subspecies, *Bubo nipalensis blighi*, is about twenty-five inches long, widely distributed but rarer than the brown wood owl, and characterized by its long ear tufts, dark upperparts, and brown-barred white underparts.

Tennent's *Sketches* includes a footnote that refers to yet another devil-bird identity. The source is a Mr. Mitford of the Ceylon Civil Service, a noted observer of this island's birds:

> *The Devil-Bird is not an owl. I never heard it until I came to Kornegalle, where it haunts the rocky hill at the back of Government house. Its ordinary note is a magnificent clear shout like that of a human being, and which can be heard at a great distance, and has a fine effect in the silence of the closing night. It has another cry like that of a hen just caught, but the sounds which have earned for it its bad name, and which I have heard but once to perfection, are indescribable, the most appalling that can be imagined, and scarcely to be heard without shuddering; I can only compare it to*

a boy in torture, whose screams are being stopped by being strangled. I have offered rewards for a specimen, but without success. The only European who had seen and fired at one agreed with the natives that it is of the size of a pigeon, with a long tail. I believe it is a Podargus or Night Hawk.

In a later note to Tennent, Mitford added:

I have since seen two birds by moonlight, one of the size and shape of a cuckoo, the other a large black bird, which I imagine to be the one which gives these calls.

In Sri Lanka, the terms "night hawk" and "podargus" refer to a number of nightjar species (related to the familiar American whippoorwill), and also their much rarer relative, the Ceylon frogmouth *Batrachostomus moniliger*. This latter species, however, can quickly be discounted as a devil-bird contender, because it only attains a diminutive total length of nine inches and is little-known even to native Sri Lankans.

Moreover, according to Drs. Salim Ali and S. Dillon Ripley in their definitive *Handbook of the Birds of India and Pakistan, Together With Those of Nepal, Sikkim, Bhutan and Ceylon* (second edition, 1969), its call consists merely of a rapid series of soft "karoo" or "whoo" cries, together with a

A frogmouth, one of the devil-bird's least likely identities.

throaty chuckle. Hardly the spine-chilling eldritch shrieks attributed to the devil-bird!

The nightjars initially appear more promising. Although equally small-bodied, their tails are much longer, so that they correspond in outline with the birds described by Mitford. Accordingly, in *A History of the Birds of Ceylon* (1880), William Vincent Legge nominated the Sri Lankan jungle nightjar *Caprimulgus indicus kelaarti* as a possible devil-bird identity. Nonetheless, their relatively restrained calls do not match those of the devil-bird. Indeed, at the present time, no known bird's do.

Nightjars—Mitford's favored devil-bird identity.

Returning to the owl identities is of little avail either. In both species, the tail is very short, and their authenticated calls once again seem too subdued for consideration. In fact, even the merest thought that the brown wood owl could be the identity of the devil-bird has been met with surprise and swift dismissal from some Sri Lankan inhabitants.

In his earlier-mentioned book, Harry Williams documented his own experiences of the devil-bird and its cry, which he described as "a gurgling, strangled shout rising to a high pitched scream which ends in a bubbling diminuendo as of a creature in its last agony." As a result, he totally rejected the Buddhists' belief that the brown wood owl was responsible for such sounds. Although his bungalow's neighboring woodlands contained many owls of this species, he never once heard that hideous cry in this area. Yet he heard it on three separate occasions in the low country jungles, which native Sri Lankans believe to be the devil-bird's home.

There is a noteworthy precedent of sorts to the mystery of Sri Lanka's devil-bird. For many years in Australia, the powerful owl *Ninox strenua* was assumed by scientists to be responsible for horrific screams reminiscent of a woman shrieking in terror; however, in more recent times the true originator of these heart-stopping cries has been exposed as a smaller relative, the barking owl *Ninox connivens*. All of this shows that the vocal abilities of some owls can indeed be more varied than popularly realized. Even so, it is very difficult to accept that so familiar and widespread a bird on Sri Lanka as the brown wood owl could be responsible for such singular cries without this behavior having been scientifically observed and verified long ago.

A further possibility to consider is whether more than one species produce the devil-bird's shrieks. That is, could the devil-bird be a composite creature, "created" by erroneously assuming that similar cries emitted by several different species are all produced by a single one? This intriguing concept was pursued in 1968 by Dr. R. L. Spittel, in a devil-bird article published by a Sri Lankan wildlife journal, *Loris*.

Spittel noted that several supposed devil-birds have actually been shot directly after emitting this mysterious form's bloodcurdling cries. When examined, however, they were found to belong to four separate species—the forest eagle owl, Sri Lankan hawk-eagle *Nisaetus cirrhatus ceylonensis*, Hodgson's hawk-eagle *Nisaetus nipalensis kelaarti*, and crested honey buzzard *Pernis ptilorhynchus ruficollis*.

One final possibility also demands attention. Many animal species have undoubtedly remained mysterious (and sometimes totally unknown to science) as a result of age-old native superstitions and taboos placed on them. Prime examples include Madagascar's lemurs. These taboos have actually been beneficial to some such creatures, protecting them from slaughter at the hands of their native human neighbors.

Consequently, it is possible that an unknown species of bird inhabits Sri Lanka's lesser-explored dense jungle lands, remaining protected from prying human eyes (and accompanying killing implements) by its fearsome cries and the superstitious horror that they have inspired. Indeed, Ali and Ripley mention that a still-undescribed form of owl belonging to the genus *Strix* apparently exists in the Andaman and Nicobar Islands. Perhaps an equally obscure owl, hawk-eagle, or even a nightjar awaits scientific recognition in Sri Lanka too.

Lastly, neither the horned jackal nor the devil-bird appears to be exclusive to Sri Lanka. India has comparable legends regarding both of these animals. There, the devil-bird is called the *churail*, according to Norah Burke, and this vast country is certainly well supplied with jackals, owls, and nightjars. So perhaps the mysteries of the horned jackal and devil-bird may ultimately be solved outside of Sri Lanka.

Nonetheless, as long as this island's prosecution lawyers can still be intimidated by an osseous oddity whose occurrence is unexplained by science, and as long as its jungles still echo with unearthly utterances more akin to those of a banshee than a bird, Sri Lanka's mystique will remain undiminished.

And even if the horned jackal and the devil-bird *are* eventually explained, there is still the nittaewo....

Six

A Horse of a Very Different Color

Blue, to Be Precise!

"…I have a strange kind of new animal—a pushmi-pullyu…."
… "Why, John Dolittle," said he, "you'll make your fortune—sure as you're alive! There's never bin anything seen like that since the world began…."

—Hugh Lofting
Doctor Dolittle's Circus

Mystery animals come in all shapes, sizes—and shades. Certainly, the following hitherto obscure example is a particularly dramatic case in point, one that could be aptly described as a horse of a different color, in every sense of the phrase.

While in South Africa during 1860, a merchant by the name of Lashmar encountered a feeding herd of quaggas—odd-looking relatives of zebras that were striped only on the front half of their body and that became extinct in 1883. As subsequently reported by C. O. G. Napier in the long-vanished English magazine *Land and Water* (February 22, 1868), while observing them Lashmar suddenly spotted in their midst a strange-looking creature that was drastically dissimilar in appearance from the others. He discovered, to his astonishment, that it was not a quagga at all, but was instead a hairless blue horse.

Once he had convinced himself that this ethereal entity was indeed real, he was quick to recognize its great worth as an outstanding novelty for exhibition purposes.

Was the mysterious hairless blue horse a freak quagga?

He thus lost no time in successfully capturing it, after which he was able to study its extraordinary appearance closely, recording the following details.

Its skin was smooth and delicate in texture, feeling to the touch like India rubber, and very warm. It formed curious wrinkles when the animal moved, calling to mind the more ornate, ostentatious creases and loose folds of skin sported by that increasingly popular breed of mastiff-related dog known as the shar-pei. Unlike the latter, however, the horse was wholly hairless, not even possessing any hair roots. In color, its skin was blue-mauve over most of its body, but with a buff face and a large patch of the same color extending over half of its back with numerous blotches. Its tail resembled that of a pig. In overall appearance and when seen at a distance, this singular steed looked as if it had been sculpted from some rare variety of oriental blue marble.

After capturing it, Lashmar sent it to South Africa's Cape Colony, from where it was brought over to England in 1863. There, it was broken in at Astley's, and ridden for three parts of the season with Lord Stamford's hounds. It was also examined by Professor Spooner of the Veterinary College, London, who delivered a lecture concerning its unique appearance to his students. Purchased by a Mr. Moffat in February 1868, it was exhibited in London's famous Crystal Palace, but its original blue coloration had gradually faded since its capture, transforming into a rather more nondescript, isabelline-gray. According to Moffat, the horse stood 14.2 hands high (that is, just under five feet tall), was symmetrically shaped, and performed well in harness, but required warm clothing on account of its hairless nature. Moffat washed it each day to keep it in good health.

Since its Crystal Palace days, nothing more seems to have been documented regarding this strange animal. Its ultimate fate, therefore, is unknown, and prior to this present account its very existence had long since been forgotten.

As an inevitable consequence of its many decades of obscurity, the reason for its bizarre appearance has never been explained. However, the creature with which it seems to correspond most closely with regard to its curious skin is the Chinese crested dog—a superficially chihuahua-like breed that is without hair over much of its body, and which has portions of blue skin coloration. This breed's hairless state is caused by the possession of a mutant form of one of the genes controlling hair development, and its blue shading arises from the presence of the pigment eumelanin in its skin. Comparable conditions in a horse could yield the type of specimen captured by Lashmar.

Needless to say, nothing like it has ever been reported since. Perhaps the only example in any way reminiscent is a mare owned by Harold T. Sills of Prospect, Dordrecht, in South Africa's Cape Colony. Unlike Lashmar's specimen, it possessed a normal coat of hair, but the hair itself was blue. Sills wrote about this animal to English naturalist William T. Tegetmeier, who published in *The Field* (August 31, 1901) the following extract from Sills' letter to him:

> I have a colonial-bred mare that is a very light blue; that is, she is nearly white, with the exception of mane, tail, and legs, which are bluish, and a black star on her forehead. The mare is about 7 years old now, and was born with this black star. It is the only case I have ever seen or heard of.

Freakish blue animals have occasionally been reported from other mammalian species, notably various wild cats, with pelts of blue lynxes and bobcats occasionally obtained by the fur trade. In southeastern China's Fujian Province, an elusive strain of blue-furred tiger allegedly existed at one time (and may still do so today). During September 1910, the renowned Methodist missionary Harry R. Caldwell actually encountered one of these extraordinary creatures at close range, and attempted to shoot it to provide unequivocal proof of its reality, but was unable to do so

A blue-furred tiger allegedly exists in China's Fujian Province.

---

because of the possibility that he might would injure two children collecting vegetation a little farther away, who were in direct line of his planned shot. An exotic white cheetah with remarkable blue spots was once brought to the Mogul naturalist Jahangir at Agra.

Nevertheless, the mystery of Lashmar's blue horse remains unsolved, and not only on account of its color and hairlessness. There is one final anomaly that seems never to have attracted attention even during this animal's brief period of celebrity status. Namely, how can we possibly explain its presence amid a herd of quaggas? Where had such a bizarre beast originally come from, and why was it now associating with a herd of creatures belonging to a wild species only distantly related to its own? Is it even conceivable that this abnormal creature was not a domestic horse at all, but was in reality a freakish mutant specimen of quagga—a sport of nature set apart from its brethren morphologically, but nevertheless recognized by them as being one of their own kind and hence permitted to feed and associate with them? Who can say?

Just like the quaggas that were themselves destined to be lost forever, there is little doubt that the secret of this strangest of all steeds died with its originator—yet another mystery beast to be reported, recorded, and afterwards conveniently forgotten like so many before, and so many since.

Seven

Giant Jellyfishes

The World's Most Dangerous Mystery Beasts?

...I had reached the deepest and stillest pool when my eyes caught that for which they were searching, and I burst into a shout of triumph.

"Cyanea!" I cried. "Cyanea! Behold the Lion's Mane!"

The strange object at which I pointed did indeed look like a tangled mass torn from the mane of a lion. It lay upon a rocky shelf some three feet under the water, a curious waving, vibrating, hairy creature with streaks of silver among its yellow tresses. It pulsated with a slow, heavy dilation and contraction.

"It has done mischief enough. Its day is over!" I cried. "Help me, Stackhurst! Let us end this nurderer for ever."

—Sir Arthur Conan Doyle
"The Adventure of the Lion's Mane"

Speculation concerning the existence of undiscovered sea monsters traditionally concentrates on sea serpents, giant octopuses, and ultra-giant squids. However, there is an additional, wholly separate category, one that is invariably overlooked during such considerations, yet whose members may well be the most dangerous mystery beasts in the world!

The Lion's Mane and the Sea Wasp

The quote that opens this chapter is taken from a Sherlock Holmes short story, and presents Holmes' own description of his dramatic encounter along a stretch of shingle in Sussex with one of the most bizarre foes ever faced by him.

The creature in question, responsible in the story for the death of a schoolmaster, was *Cyanea capillata*, the lion's mane jellyfish, whose Arctic form is the world's largest

Do giant, undiscovered jellyfishes lurk in the world's oceans?

known type of jellyfish. One immense specimen, recorded from Massachusetts Bay in 1865, had a bell diameter of sevenand a half feet, and gigantic tentacles stretching 120 feet, thereby yielding a tentacle spread of about 245 feet. Bearing in mind that each such jellyfish has numerous tentacles, and each tentacle is ringed by thousands of stinging and paralyzing cells called nematocysts, contact with such a monster by an unwary swimmer could prove extremely dangerous.

As yet, no human fatality has been formally recorded with this particular type (notwithstanding Sherlock Holmes' account!). Yet there are smaller species whose nematocyst toxin is much more potent, and for which human fatalities have indeed been confirmed. The most notorious of these killers is Flecker's sea wasp *Chironex fleckeri* from Australia, whose sting is so agonizing that it is claimed to be the most excruciating pain known to humanity. Some of its victims have died in convulsions of screaming insanity caused by the unrelenting agony that can result from even the briefest of skin contact with its tentacles' nematocysts.

Remarkably, this terrible creature remained completely unknown to science until as recently as 1956. Even more astounding is the likelihood that in the depths of the sea are still-unknown giant jellyfishes whose stings could well rival those of *Chironex*. This fearsome possibility is raised by various little-publicized eyewitness accounts, which are now brought together here for cryptozoological investigation for the first time.

Trapped by the Tentacles of Terror

One of the most dramatic cases on record was documented by James Sweeney in *Sea Monsters* (1977), and took place in January 1973. While sailing toward the Fijian Islands from Australia, the 1,483-ton sea vessel *Kuranda* encountered some very turbulent waves. While navigating through them, the front portion of the ship dipped down into the water and seemed to collide with something beneath the surface. When the ship's bow re-emerged, the crew was horrified to perceive a colossal jellyfish, weighing at least twenty tons, draped all over the entire forecastle head.

Clearly the object into which the *Kuranda* had collided, this monstrous, animated glob began thrashing its enormously long tentacles across the deck. To the terrified eyewitnesses, it must have resembled a hideous disembodied gorgon's head, with countless serpents for hair lashing out venomously in all directions. One unfortunate crew member came within range of these deadly tentacles, which instantly adhered to his skin. He was pulled clear by other seamen on board, but the tentacles had seared into his flesh so severely that, according to one eyewitness, he looked as if he had been scalded by steam.

As if the danger posed by this creature's tentacles was not enough, an additional threat was conferred by virtue of its colossal bulk, which seemed likely to send the *Kuranda* plunging down to the sea bottom. According to the *Kuranda's* captain, Langley Smith, the deck was awash in a two-foot-deep mass of tentacular slime, and some of the tentacles themselves were estimated to be at least 200 feet long.

Frantically, the crew did their best to clear the deck of this gelatinous horror, but its formidable stinging capability deterred every attempt made. If they needed any further proof of its deadly potency, the seaman who had been stung earlier had by now died from his injuries.

This frightening episode could well have ended in even greater tragedy, but happily an S.O.S. put out by the *Kuranda* was detected by the *Hercules*, a deep-sea salvage tug 500 miles away, which set out at once to offer whatever assistance it could. The dreadful sight of the stupendous jellyfish enveloping a sizeable proportion of the *Kuranda* met the near-unbelieving eyes of the *Hercules* crew when they drew near, but with the aid of two high-pressure hoses spraying steam directly at the creature, it was eventually dislodged.

Following the *Kuranda's* arrival back in Sydney, samples of the jellyfish's gelatinous slime were formally analyzed, and the specimen from which they were derived was tentatively identified as a lion's mane—but one of incomparably huge proportions.

From Bermuda to Baiselle

Another immense (but seemingly less belligerent) jellyfish monster had come to notice three years earlier. In November 1969, skin divers Richard Winer and Pat Boatwright encountered an almost round, gigantic object pulsating beneath them at a depth of 100 to 150 feet, while they were diving in waters fourteen miles southwest of Bermuda. As later reported by Gary Mangiacopra (*Of Sea and Shore*, fall 1976), the mysterious entity had a diameter of fifty to a hundred feet, and was deep purple with a pink-shaded outer rim. As they observed it, the creature slowly drifted up through the water towards them, inducing the divers to begin their own ascent with all speed. Their pursuer paused, then began descending once more.

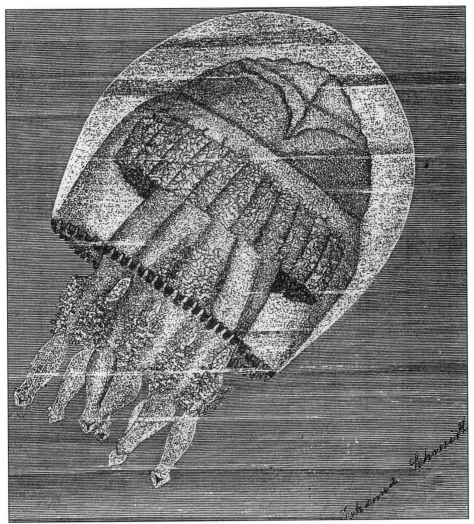

Rhizostoma—a near spherical jellyfish.

What must surely be the most controversial giant jellyfish case on file featured one such monster's supposed engulfing of the two children and wife of French fisherman Henri Baiselle while they were swimming with him in the sea near Bordeaux during the late 1980s. Not too surprisingly, Baiselle's account of a huge jellyfish the size of a car that swallowed up his family before sinking out of sight failed to prevent the local police from arresting him on a murder charge, but he passed a lie detector test and refused to change his story (*Fortean Times*, fall 1990).

What Eats the Sharks?

So far, the jellyfishes reported have been fairly typical in shape, if not in size, but there is one very macabre mystery beast on record that may well be a scientifically unknown representative of one of their more specialized, deepwater forms. This is the singularly eerie creature spied in 1953 by an Australian diver while testing a new type of deep-sea diving suit in the South Pacific.

As revealed by Eric Frank Russell in his book *Great World Mysteries* (1957), the diver had been following a shark, and was resting on the edge of a chasm leading down to much deeper depths. He was still watching the shark when an immense, dull brown, shapeless mass rose up out of the chasm, pulsating sluggishly, and flat in general outline with ragged edges.

Despite appearing devoid of eyes or other instantly recognizable sensory organs, this malign presence evidently discerned the shark's presence somehow, because it floated upwards until its upper surface made direct contact. The shark instantly gave a convulsive shudder, and was then drawn without resistance into the hideous monster's body. After that, the creature sank back down into the chasm, leaving behind a very frightened diver to ponder what might have happened if that nightmarish, nameless entity had not been attracted to the shark.

In the past, a deep-sea octopus has been put forward as a possible identity for this disturbing creature, but in reality a deep-sea jellyfish is a much more plausible candidate. To begin with, all octopuses have tentacles, but a number of jellyfishes (including various known deep-sea species) do not. However, *all* jellyfishes are armed with nematocysts (sometimes on their body surface as well as on their tentacles), which in some species, as noted earlier, can elicit paralysis or indescribable pain. Accordingly, if the amorphous creature observed by the diver was equipped with a plentiful supply of these, the immediate paralysis of the shark could be readily explained.

In addition, though the shark's killer lacked such obvious sensory organs as eyes (this is true of all jellyfishes), its ability to detect the shark can again be explained via the jellyfish identity. These animals possess primitive sensory structures receptive to water movements. Hence the creature would have been able to detect the water disturbances created by the shark's swimming. How fortunate it was, therefore, that by choosing to watch the shark, the diver had remained stationary.

Is the sinister shark-stunner a deep-sea jellyfish?

The Hidden Hide of Chile

Deep-sea jellyfishes similar (though not identical) to the aforementioned creature encountered by the diver may explain Chilean legends of a grotesque sea monster termed the *hide*, documented by Jorge Luis Borges in his famous work *The Book of Imaginary Beings* (1969). According to Borges, the hide is an octopus that resembles in shape and size a cowhide stretched out flat, with countless eyes all around its body's perimeter, and four larger ones in the center. It lives by rising to the surface of the sea and swallowing any animals, or people, swimming there.

As this description makes no mention of tentacles, it seems highly unlikely that such a beast (assuming that it really does exist) could be any

The familiar moon jellyfish.

form of octopus. In any event, octopuses only have a single pair of eyes, not a whole series around the edge of their body and *two* pairs of principal eyes. Conversely, many jellyfishes possess peripheral sensory organs called rhopalia, which incorporate simple light-sensitive eyespots or ocelli. Moreover, although no jellyfish has true eyes, some—such as the common moon jellyfish *Aurelia aurita*—have four deceptively eye-like organs visible in the center of their bell (which are actually portions of their gut, known as gastric pouches). In short, a jellyfish candidate provides a far more realistic answer to the question of the hide's identity than an octopus.

It would be unwise to dismiss out of hand the possibility that jellyfishes notably larger than any recorded so far by science exist in our world's vast oceans. However, most may well frequent the abyssal depths, where man has scarcely begun to penetrate.

Consequently, as indicated by the cases reviewed here, it would seem that we will only learn more about these least-known, yet potentially most lethal, sea monsters when they themselves choose to make their presence felt. Bearing in mind the outcomes of certain such visitations in the past, however, perhaps even the most ardent cryptozoologists will concede that it may be better for such beasts to remain in quiescent, sea-bottom anonymity indefinitely.

Eight

Here Be Dragons

Or Something Quite Like Them

Dragons! Fire-belching damsel devourers mortally skewered upon a valiant knight's lance, or ethereal serpentine deities wafting languorously through the skies in celestial tranquillity. Vermiform monsters with coils of steel, or winged wonders with jewel-encrusted scales. Bat-winged nightmares that terrorize and desecrate with volcanic gullets of flame, or polychromatic dream beasts soaring heavenward upon iridescent plumes of crystalline glory. Personifications of malevolence or beneficence, paganism or purity, death and devastation, life and fertility, good or evil. All of these varied, contradictory concepts are embodied and embedded within that single magical word.

—**Dr. Karl P. N. Shuker**
Dragons: A Natural History

The giant-sized, fire-spewing dragons of myth and folklore appear to have no direct zoological counterparts to account for their legends' origins, but what about the many rather smaller, less spectacular dragons also featured in these tales? Some of their models were undoubtedly such familiar, real animals as large snakes, lizards, and crocodiles. Certain others, however, may well have been various elusive dragon-like beasts that still elude formal scientific recognition even today. This chapter surveys a thought-provoking selection of reports featuring undiscovered or unaccepted reptilian monsters from around the world. Put another way, here be dragons—or something quite like them.

Are dragons more than creatures of myth and folktale?

Drake and the Dragon: New Guinea's Ambiguous Artrellia

Since the end of the nineteenth century, reports of gigantic, arboreal drag-ons have been emerging quite regularly from Papua, the eastern section of New Guinea. Said to be up to thirty feet long and given to dropping down from overhanging branches onto unsuspecting creatures (and sometimes humans) walking underneath, they are termed the *artrellia* by the New Guinea natives—who, understandably, live in considerable fear of these great beasts, and liken them to giant crocodiles or lizard-like creatures. Many Westerners have also seen them.

In World War II, for example, a number of soldiers stationed in Papua claimed to have spied huge lizards estimated at fifteen to twenty feet in length. Similarly, in 1960 David Marsh (at that time District Commissioner of Port Moresby, Papua's capital) said that he had made two sightings of such reptiles during the early 1940s in western Papua. Also in 1960, two administration agricultural officers, Lindsay Green and Fred Kleckhan, suc-ceeded in obtaining the skin and jawbone of a New Guinea "dragon"; they had discovered these relics in a native village near Kairuku, seventy miles northwest of Port Moresby.

The trail of the artrellia was growing ever warmer, and fresh findings con-tinued to be made as the years rolled by. In *Journey Into the Stone Age* (1969), traveler David M. Davies recalled being shown by some valley-inhabiting Papuans an unusual native drawing on a wall, which appeared to depict a huge lizard running on its hind legs, and of which his native companions were evidently very afraid. A major breakthrough occurred less than a decade later when, in late 1978, news emerged concerning the successful filming of a New Guinea dragon, one of a population of such creatures found in southern Papua, by Jean Becker and Christian Meyer. However, it was still not clear whether these composed a new species.

That issue was finally resolved in early 1980, during an "Operation Drake" expedition to the Papuan swamplands, led by intrepid explorer Lieutenant Colonel John Blashford-Snell. As he documented in his book *Mysteries: Encounters With the Unexplained* (1983), he had heard numerous native stories of these enormous beasts, and was regaled with tales of their ferocity and the danger to anyone seeking to capture one. Notwithstanding this, Blashford-Snell was so intrigued by these reports that he became determined to resolve this longstanding zoological mystery once and for all—by revealing conclusively the identity of New Guinea's dragon.

Sadly, however, his own expedition's attempts to achieve this met with failure, and the natives were very loathe to participate in the pursuit, until he resorted to an age-old but universally successful ploy: he bribed them. Sure enough, before many days had passed, he was duly presented with a real-life artrellia. True, it was far from the thirty-foot monster that Blashford-Snell had been expecting, measuring instead a mere six feet, one and a half inches. Nevertheless, the natives were still palpably nervous of this mini-dragon, and assured him unhesitatingly that it was a genuine artrellia, albeit a very young one.

When his zoological colleagues examined it, they recognized its species at once. It was an arboreal lizard called *Varanus salvadorii*, Salvadori's monitor, not to be confused (though it often is) with the closely related salvator monitor *Varanus salvator*. Moreover, they confirmed that this was indeed only a very immature specimen, so to what size could fully adult ones grow? Handsomely marked with black and gold spots, and equipped with a fiery-colored flame-thrower facsimile of a tongue continually flicking in and out of its mouth in faithful homage to those conflagrating dragons of legend, this impressive species is known from fully confirmed records to exceed ten feet in total length quite regularly when adult, thereby making it the longest species of lizard in the world.

Based on the vast number of reports describing quite immense artrellias in New Guinea, however, it would seem that Salvadori's monitor can far exceed even the longest officially verified record for its species—fifteen feet, seven inches, recorded from a male specimen measured some time ago by researcher Michael Pope.

Worth noting here, incidentally, is that the title of the world's longest species of lizard is often, but erroneously, ascribed to a famous relative of Salvadori's monitor—the Komodo dragon *Varanus komodoensis*. In reality, however, the Komodo dragon is *not* the longest (it rarely exceeds ten feet), but it *is* the largest. The reason for this distinction is that whereas at least two-thirds of the total length of Salvadori's monitor is composed of its very slender tail, the tail of the Komodo dragon only accounts for half of its total length , which makes the Komodo dragon much sturdier and heavier than the svelte, lightweight Salvadori's monitor.

So far, no one has captured a thrity-foot artrellia, but sightings continue. Certainly it is plausible that in the more remote jungles and swamps of New Guinea (of which there are a very great many still in need of scientific investigation), little frequented by man, and hence constituting sanctuaries for larger forms of life, specimens of artrellia at the upper end of their species' scale of dimensions do exist, undisturbed and free from human persecution. Moreover, many species of monitor will often run on their hind legs alone, should the need arise. This could explain the drawing reported by David M. Davies.

Drakensberg's Das-Adder: A Hyrax-Headed Hypnotist

Also known as conies or dassies, and native to many parts of Africa, hyraxes are small, rabbit-like hoofed mammals whose closest relatives are the mighty elephants. According to more than a century's worth of reports and alleged sightings, they also appear to share some degree of similarity with a very different creature believed by many to inhabit the appropriately named Drakensberg ("Dragon's Mountain") Range, in South Africa.

This extraordinary beast is commonly referred to as the das-adder or dassie-adder, because it supposedly combines a hyrax-like head with the sinuous body of a viper-like snake. Many natives firmly believe it to be extremely venomous, and capable of luring a person within reach of its deadly jaws by fixing him with its irresistible, mesmeric gaze.

In a detailed account of African mystery beasts (*Empire Review*, 1940), W. L. Speight noted that the skin around the das-adder's external ear openings was folded into a crest, and that it bears red and yellow stripes on its tail, similar to those of the puff adder. He also mentioned that some authorities consider it not to be any form of snake at all, but rather a type of lizard whose tail measures as much as two feet in length.

No specimen confirmed by locals to be a genuine das-adder has so far been submitted to science for official identification. As far back as the early nineteenth century Dr. Andrew Smith of Cape Town Museum advertised in vain for one. Nowadays, most reptile researchers dismiss sightings of the das-adder, claiming that they are based on nothing more startling than poorly glimpsed specimens of the Cape rock monitor *Varanus albigularis*.

Native to the more stony, arid regions of South Africa, when viewed in the open the identity of this species as a large, four-foot-long lizard cannot be doubted. As pointed out in his book *Snakes* (1932) by former snake curator Dr. F. W. Fitzsimons, however, when viewed slipping between rocks and boulders it might well be mistaken for a large adder.

Even so, the head of a monitor lizard bears scant resemblance to a hyrax's, and although *V. albigularis* does have a long tail, its body is not patterned with red and yellow stripes. So perhaps the mystery of the das-adder has still to be conclusively resolved after all.

The Cape rock monitor—identity of the das-adder?

The bizarre cat-headed snake of Frumsemberg Mountain.

Mammal-headed snakes are not confined to Africa either. Reports of bizarre cat-headed serpents have emerged from Central Europe's Alps for centuries. One such beast, measuring seven feet long, was supposedly shot dead (but not preserved) in or around 1711 by Jean Tinner and his father at Hauwelen on Switzerland's Frumsemberg Mountain. Another feline-headed elongate beast, but with two front limbs, reputedly attacked a herd of pigs near Palermo, Sicily, in 1954. Perhaps this was a southern version of the equally mysterious *tatzelworm*, a large but still-unidentified, two-legged reptilian creature again reported from the Alps.

Do giant horned lizards exist in British Columbia?

The Horned Horrors of British Columbia

According to a report in the *Vancouver Province* newspaper for May 12, 1978 (reprinted in *Res Bureaux Bulletin*), woodsman Warren Scott claimed that he and his wife had seen a number of strange lizard-like beasts, measuring up to five feet in length and equipped with horns and sharp teeth, in a secluded valley, just under two miles long, near Pitt Lake, British Columbia. Scott also asserted that he actually caught some smaller specimens of this unidentified species and sent one, preserved in alcohol, to the Simon Fraser University's biology department. In reply, however, the department's staff stated that they had no record of receiving such a specimen. A frustrating but hardly unprecedented situation; there are all too many similar cases on file testifying to the unsettling fact that cryptozoological creatures have an alarming tendency to remain elusive even when dead.

The Gowrow and the Devil's Hole

For more than a century, inhabitants of rural Arkansas have spoken of a twenty-foot-long tusked lizard called the *gowrow*, reputedly lurking within caverns and under rock ledges. In 1897, one was supposedly killed near

Marshall by traveling salesman William Miller, who claimed that he dispatched its carcass to the Smithsonian Institution, but there is no record of its arrival.

Sometime prior to 1935, near the village of Self in Boone County, a gowrow allegedly inhabited the Devil's Hole, a deep cave whose mouth opened on the estate of E. J. Rhodes. One day, after hearing a commotion emanating from Devil's Hole's underground recesses, Rhodes decided to investigate by lowering himself into its shaft and descending via rope to a ledge 200 feet beneath the opening. Below this point, the shaft was too narrow to permit further descent, so Rhodes failed to satisfy his curiosity—which was probably just as well. When some men lowered a flatiron, attached to a rope, down the shaft to the same level that Rhodes had reached, a loud angry hissing noise could be plainly heard. They heard it again when they repeated the procedure, this time using a large stone attached to the rope. Moreover, when they drew the rope back up they discovered that the stone was gone. The section of the rope holding it had been completely bitten through!

Could the *gowrow* be more than a fanciful folk story?

Indian Bis-Cobras and Lizards with Hair

The only venomous lizards known to science are the Gila monster *Heloderma suspectum* (native to the southwestern U.S.A. and northwestern Mexico) and its relative the Mexican beaded lizard, *H. horridum*. In northern India, however, natives greatly fear a reputedly venomous mystery lizard, which they call the *bis-cobra*, because it supposedly possesses the killing power of twenty cobras.

The bis-cobra is sometimes classed as one or more of this area's lizard species already known to science (particularly various of the agamas, and also the gecko *Eublepharis hardwickei*), but according to local testimony it is differentiated from all such lizards by its deadly bite and the formidable ability to spit its lethal venom at any potential assailant.

As with such morphologically diverse mystery beasts as the "great sea serpent" and the Nandi bear, the bis-cobra is probably another non-existent composite creature, "created" by the mistaken grouping together of reports referring to several wholly separate types of lizard—though these types may include one or more that are genuinely unknown to science. Also needing to be taken into consideration here is the frequent tendency to endow with venomous potentiality any creature that people dislike or fear. Reptiles consistently feature very significantly, on a worldwide basis, in people's lists of unpopular animals.

On April 17, 1906, while leading an expedition on foot through New Guinea towards Mount Albert Edward, Captain Charles Monckton stopped off at a gold-digging site on the Aikora River. Speaking with the two men working the claim, he learned that their operation had disclosed some small caves. They had later washed out several strange beasts that resembled large lizards, but with hairy or furry skins. Unfortunately, the men had not preserved any of them, and during his stay Monckton did not succeed in obtaining one. Upon his departure, he left behind a small tank of preserving fluid in case the men should ever come upon any more of these remarkable reptiles, but none was seen again.

On the Trail of the Row: An Adventure in Muddled Morphology?

During the 1940s, explorer Charles Miller and his wife Leona visited the Sterren Mountains of New Guinea, where they allegedly encountered not only a hitherto-unknown tribe of cannibals called the Kirrirri, but also what

Miller believed to be a living dinosaur. Their introduction to this latter beast came about in a somewhat unusual manner—courtesy of a coconut de-husker used by one of the native women.

Leona noticed that the tool in question, roughly eighteen inches long and twenty pounds in weight, resembled the distal portion of an elephant tusk or rhino horn. However, because there are no elephants or rhinos in New Guinea, she was perplexed as to its true identity and origin. When she told her husband, he made some inquiries and was shown several of these curious objects, which were made of a horn-like substance present in cone-shaped layers; they resembled a stacked pile of paper drinking cups, one cup inside another. When pressed for more details, some of the natives drew a strange lizard-like creature in the sand, whose tail terminated in one of these horns. They called this beast the *row* (after its loud cry), and said that it was forty feet long.

Although Miller was initially skeptical of their claims, he could not deny the evidence of the horns and could offer no alternative explanation for their origin. When he learned that the hills to the northwest of the Kirrirri camp reputedly harbored these gigantic beasts, he set out with his wife and a native party in the hope of filming them. After a couple days' journey, they reached a triangular swamp situated between two plateaux and occupying an area of roughly forty acres. As Miller sat there, looking at a bed of tall reeds a quarter of a mile away, the reeds suddenly moved. Something was behind them. Hardly daring to breathe, Miller waited for them to move again, camera in hand. When they did, the result was so shocking that Leona collapsed to the ground, almost fainting with fear.

A long, thin neck bearing a small head fringed with a flaring bony hood had risen up through the reeds, followed by a sturdy elephantine body bearing a series of huge triangular plates running along its backbone, and a lengthy tapering tail bearing at its tip one of the mysterious horns that Miller had come to know so well. Its front limbs were shorter than its hind limbs, and while Miller was filming it, the row unexpectedly paused, raised itself up onto its hind limbs, and peered in the party's direction, almost as if it sensed the presence of these human interlopers in its private, prehistoric domain. In color, it was precisely the same shade of light yellow-brown as the surrounding reeds, no doubt affording it excellent camouflage should it seek anonymity, but it was presently intent on more extrovert behavior, rearing up on two further occasions before disappearing from sight behind a clump of dwarf eucalyptus trees, just as Miller's film ran out.

In 1950, his extraordinary adventure was published in book form as *Cannibal Caravan*. Yet despite containing many interesting pictures, there was

Even to cryptozoologists, the *row* may seem as likely as meeting a living dinosaur in the high street!

none of his most spectacular discovery, the row. There was not even a photo of one of the horns. Similarly, although Miller claimed to have shown the film to various (unnamed) authorities, nothing more has ever emerged regarding it. Perhaps the most paradoxical aspect of this entire episode, however, concerns the row itself. Although palaeontologists currently recognize the former existence of several hundred different species of dinosaurs, collectively yielding a myriad of shapes, sizes, and forms, not one compares even superficially with the row—for very good reason. As cryptozoologist Dr. Bernard Heuvelmans pointed out in *On the Track of Unknown Animals* (1958), the row's morphology is little short of surrealistic, because it combines the characteristics of several wholly unrelated groups of dinosaurs.

Little wonder, then, why cryptozoologists are reluctant to countenance any likelihood of this ostensibly composite creature's reality. Of course, their denunciation could be premature, but as long as Miller's film remains as elusive as the beast that it allegedly depicts, how can we blame them for remaining unconvinced?

Flying Dragons or Living Pterosaurs?

Many cryptozoological publications have included eyewitness accounts of mysterious winged dragon-like beasts reported from Africa and the U.S.A. that resemble living representatives of those familiar flying reptiles from prehistory known as pterosaurs, typified by the pterodactyls. Less well known, however, is that these creatures' files also contain several reports emanating from far beyond those geographical confines.

J. Richard Greenwell, secretary of the International Society of Cryptozoology, has a Mexican correspondent who claims that there are living pterosaurs in eastern Mexico and is determined to capture one, to prove beyond any shadow of a doubt that they do exist. Worthy of note is that certain depictions of deities, demons, and strange beasts from ancient Mexican mythology are decidedly pterodactylian in appearance. One particularly intriguing example is the mysterious "serpent-bird" portrayed in relief sculpture amid the Mayan ruins of Tajin, in Veracruz's northeastern portion, noted in 1968 by visiting Mexican archaeologist Dr. José Diaz-Bolio, and dating from a mere 1,000 to 5,000 years ago. Yet all pterosaurs had officially become extinct at least sixty-four million years ago. So how do we explain the Mayan serpent-bird—a non-existent, imaginary beast, or a creature lingering long after its formal date of demise? Although neither solution would be unprecedented, only one is correct. But which one?

Around February 1947, J. Harrison from Liverpool was on a boat navigating an estuary of the Amazon river when he and some others aboard spied a flock of five huge birds flying overhead in "V" formation, with long necks and beaks, and each with a wingspan of about twelve feet. According to Harrison, however, their wings resembled brown leather and appeared to be featherless. As they soared down the river, he could see that their heads were flat on top, and the wings seemed to be ribbed. Judging from the sketch that he prepared, however, they bore little resemblance to pterosaurs, and were far more reminiscent of a large stork, three of which, the jabiru, maguari, and wood ibis, are native here.

A bird is also more likely than a pterosaur to be the explanation for the blue-winged red "pterodactyl" spied flying with an undulating motion over a new motorway in New Zealand sometime prior to 1982. If such a conspicuously colored beast was markedly pterosaurian in appearance, there would surely have been other sightings on record, but none has so far been brought to cryptozoological attention.

One morning in July 1987 or thereabouts, near a small river in Crete's Asteroussia Mountains, three youngsters allegedly spied what looked at first like a giant dark gray bird flying low towards the mountains. As it approached them, however, they could see that its wings were membranous, like those of a bat, with finger-like projections. It also had a pelican-like beak and clawed feet. After poring through several books, they learned that the animal bearing the closest resemblance to their mystery beast was the pterodactyl.

Last and least is the infamous French pterodactyl that supposedly emerged, weak but nonetheless alive, from out of a hollow boulder blasted apart during the excavation of a new railway tunnel at Culmout, according to an *Illustrated London News* report for February 9, 1856. As soon as it took its first breath of air, however, it promptly expired. Here, therefore, was a true prehistoric survivor—not a modern-day descendant of an ancient line, but a bona fide prehistoric creature that had somehow survived in suspended animation for more than sixty-four million years. When its body was examined by an anonymous expert, he was able to identify its species very precisely—*Pterodactylus anas*. Yet, amazingly, nothing more was ever heard of this zoologically priceless specimen.

In reality, of course, there is no such species, and there was no such specimen either, but none of this should come as any surprise to the linguistically minded, for whom all of the clues for deciphering the true nature of this tall tale are readily available. After all, "anas" is Latin for "duck," which in French (the pterodactyl was found in France) is *canard*—a word with a very different meaning in English!

Unmasking the Oldeani Monster

To the chagrin of cryptozoologists and the delight of their critics, the conclusive identification of a longstanding mystery beast is not a common occurrence. That is why, to close this chapter on would-be dragons, I have particular pleasure in including (for the very first time in print) one such revelation that I was personally able to achieve.

As documented in the first volume of his *Travel Diaries of a Naturalist* (1983), on February 25, 1962, world-renowned conservationist and naturalist Sir Peter Scott, during a visit to Africa, set off for Tanzania's Serengeti Plains with companions John and Jane Hunter from their home at Oldeani. They had reached the Ngorongoro Conservation Authority Area when they spied a large, unfamiliar-looking chameleon crossing the road just beyond the Area's entrance.

Somewhat elongate in shape with a lengthy tail, and a tiny horn at the tip of its snout, this mysterious lizard was brown in basic color, with small red spots and a distinctive horizontal stripe running across the center of each flank. It was probably a male. Later the creature was nicknamed the Oldeani monster

Scott was so intrigued that he picked up this "monster," which promptly attempted to bite him. Undeterred, he took it back home with him when he returned to England, where it lived for eighteen months at his famous Wildfowl Trust at Slimbridge. When it died, its body was preserved and Scott referred it to several herpetological experts in the hope of identifying its species. However, no one could offer a satisfactory answer.

One authority suggested that it may actually be a female, not a male, and related to *Chamaeleo jacksonii merumontana*, a subspecies of the distinctly dragonesque Jackson's chameleon. Another considered the possibility that it was a juvenile of an extremely large species called Meller's chameleon C. *melleri*, but this was later disproved. Scott himself was inclined to believe that it belonged to a hitherto-undescribed species, and even proposed *Chamaeleo oldeanii* as a suitable name.

The Oldeani monster, as painted by Sir Peter Scott in his diary.

Tragically, however, the bottle containing the earthly remains of the obscure Oldeani monster was eventually lost, possibly destroyed inadvertently. Consequently, it seemed as if the mystery of its identity could never be solved.

At the beginning of 1991, however, after reading Scott's book, I became very interested in the Oldeani monster, and set about seeking an answer to this longstanding riddle myself.

First of all, I sent details of its history to herpetologist Colin McCarthy at London's Natural History Museum. In response, I learned from him that the expert who had nominated *Chamaeleo jacksonii merumontana* as a likely identity for this specimen was chameleon specialist Dr. Dick Hillenius, at Amsterdam University's Institute for Taxonomic Zoology, who had seen some color transparencies of the Oldeani monster sent by Scott to the Natural History Museum in April 1983.

I then contacted Scott's widow, Lady Philippa Scott, who confirmed that the Oldeani monster's remains had never been found again, but she did have some color transparencies of it. She also commented that it had seemed very similar to the two-banded chameleon *Chamaeleo bitaeniatus*.

In November 1991, after reading a cryptozoological article by him in *Tier und Museum*, I wrote to German herpetologist Dr. Wolfgang Böhme, who has a great interest in mystery reptiles. Indeed, he is famous for unveiling a hitherto-unknown species of monitor lizard, now known as the Yemen monitor *Varanus yemenensis*, while in the comfort of his own home. Viewing a TV documentary concerning Yemen one evening in 1985, he spotted a strange-looking monitor in it; his subsequent investigations confirmed that its species was totally new to science.

After reading my letter, the mystery of the Oldeani monster was a mystery no longer either. Böhme recognized its species immediately, naming it as *Bradypodion uthmoelleri*. Moreover, in the journal *Salamandra* (December 15, 1990), he had actually published a paper dealing with this latter lizard. It is an exceedingly rare species, formally described by science in 1938, but as recently as 1990, it was known from just three specimens—the latest of these being the first recorded female, collected from the Ngorongoro crater.

Happily, my own interest in the Oldeani monster had forged the vital link between two discrete parties with complementary information. Namely, Lady Scott, with firsthand knowledge of the Oldeani monster, but not of Böhme's paper; and Böhme, with firsthand knowledge of *Bradypodion uthmoelleri*, but not of the Oldeani monster, which was a previously unrecognized, fourth specimen of this reclusive species.

After almost three decades, the remains of the Oldeani monster can at last rest in peace, wherever they are.

Nine

How Dead Is the Dodo?

When Did It Really Die Out?

> *If there are no longer any dodos…on the three Mascarene islands, must we conclude that it is absolutely impossible that there could be present-day survivors? Not as long as unexplored and uninhabited islands exist in the Indian Ocean in the general vicinity of the areas where these birds once existed.*
>
> **—Professor Roy P. Mackal**
> *Searching for Hidden Animals*

The Indian Ocean's Mascarene Islands—Mauritius, Reunion, and Rodriguez—have acquired everlasting fame as the former homes of one of the world's most celebrated and curious families of extinct birds. I refer, of course, to those flightless hook-billed pigeons of gargantuan stature and appearance known to zoologists as the Raphidae, but known to everyone else as the dodos.

The dodo of Mauritius, *Raphus cucullatus*, has become the modern-day epitome of obsolescence. "As dead as the dodo" is the ultimate phrase used to describe anything, avian or otherwise, that is irrevocably dated, destroyed, or deceased.

The most ironic aspect of the dodos' extinction is that at one time there was every opportunity to save them. Quite a number of dodos were brought back to Europe, and unlike so many of the tropics' much more delicate avifauna they appeared to be physiologically robust. Indeed, as David Day remarks in *The Doomsday Book of Animals* (1981), any birds that could survive the rough sea voyages of the seventeenth century had to be tough.

**Has the dodo
really died out?**

Furthermore, some apparently survived for a number of years in their new European homes. If serious attempts had been made to save them by captive breeding, the existence of these Alice in Wonderland birds within today's parklands and gardens may well have been a firm reality instead of an intangible romantic fantasy. Yet no such attempt was made.

Instead, the Mauritius dodo is generally believed to have died out in 1681. Moreover, both of this species' Mascarene relatives—the solitaires of Reunion, *Raphus solitarius,* and Rodriguez, *Pezophaps solitaria*—apparently followed it into oblivion by the latter part of the eighteenth century. Some ornithologists claim that a second species of true dodo may also have once existed; dubbed *Victoriornis imperialis* and reported from Reunion, this controversial form supposedly became extinct around 1770.

Yet is it possible that some dodos, and perhaps solitaires, too, survived well beyond their officially recognized dates of extinction, persisting into much more recent times? As it happens, there are two very different but equally intriguing and pertinent tie-ins to this tantalizing question.

The solitaire of Rodriguez.

The Dodo of Nazareth

The first of these tie-ins, brought to light in modern times through the researches of Willy Ley and the subsequent attention that they received from Professor Roy P. Mackal, is concerned with the geography of the dodo's former territory.

Although Mauritius, Reunion, and Rodriguez are without doubt the most familiar, they are not the only islands contained within this particular expanse of the Indian Ocean. To the north of these three major islands lie many smaller and less familiar ones, most of which have never been explored or even inhabited by man. Yet at least one could be of considerable significance to the possibility of recent dodo survival.

In 1638, French explorer François Cauche led an expedition to Mauritius and later wrote a detailed account of his adventures. In it, he referred to *oiseaux de Nazaret* ("birds of Nazareth") in relation to dodos. Consequently, several subsequent books included mention of a new species called *Didus nazarenus*—the Nazareth dodo. But where was Nazareth? What exactly did it mean? Was it the name of some mysterious island? Could it have been merely a mistranslation of some descriptive phrase used in connection with ordinary dodos? It was all most bewildering.

Much more recently, in his *The Lungfish and the Unicorn* (1941), Willy Ley, a scientist much interested in cryptozoology, re-examined the confusing case of the Nazareth dodo and favored the latter explanation as the most likely solution.

The first European explorers of Mauritius were Dutch, and these had referred to the dodos as *Walghvogel* ("nauseating birds"), on account of their inedible flesh. Ley observed that the translation of this into French was *oiseaux de nausée*, which sounds similar to *oiseaux de Nazaret*. Added to this is the fact that Ley could find no evidence (at first) for the existence of a Nazareth Island, except for a few ancient maps carrying the name. Ley dismissed its presence on these as nothing more than a synonym for one of the major Mascarene islands. However, the position of "Nazareth Island" as marked on these maps did not correspond with the known location of any of the major Mascarenes—a puzzling inconsistency that Ley explained away as cartographical inaccuracy.

So, according to Ley, Cauche had mistaken oiseaux de nausée for oiseaux de Nazaret, with Nazareth being nothing more than an alternative name for one of the principal Mascarenes. All of this was eminently plausible, until, as he would show in his later book *Exotic Zoology* (1959), Ley discovered that a Nazareth Island totally separate from these latter islands really did exist.

It turned out that this was the name early Portugese sailors had given to a tiny islet called the Ile Tromelin. Of 54°25′ E longitude and 15°51′ S latitude according to *The Times Atlas of the World: Comprehensive Edition* (1996), this is a remote, diminutive island (less than three miles long) lying approximately 375 miles northwest of Mauritius, 250 miles east of Madagascar, and sited within the Mascarene Basin. Even more stimulating than his identification of Tromelin as the mysterious Nazareth Island, however, was Ley's discovery that the nineteenth-century dodo expert Anthonie

Cornelius Oudemans had suggested that Tromelin may be worth exploring in search of fossil (and even living) dodos.

As he noted in a full report in his *Searching for Hidden Animals* (1980), Professor Roy Mackal, vice-president of the International Society of Cryptozoology (ISC), has followed up the history of the Nazareth dodos and Ley's corresponding research very closely.

Intrigued by the zoological potential ascribed to Tromelin by Oudemans, Professor Mackal set out to learn more about this mysterious islet. He discovered from a nautical chart depicting the isle (produced from a Madagascan survey of the area carried out in 1959) that its only links with humanity are its ownership by France and its possession of a small airstrip plus a meteorological station (apparently of automatic type). Nothing seems to be known of its wildlife.

Many other comparably tiny and insignificant islands exist in this area. Most remain scientifically unexplored or unnoticed. As Mackal notes, this is no doubt due at least in part to the existence of treacherous reefs and shoals that would make any attempt at landing on these islands hazardous in the extreme. At least twenty such islands, none more than a square kilometer in area, make up the Cargados Carajos Shoals, which are primarily fishing stations. Then there are the two Agalega Islands, connected by a sandbar and covered with coconut palms, which are again used for fishing. But what of their wildlife?

Relative to the Cargados Shoals, Mackal reports that as many as a dozen of these islands may house zoological and botanical surprises. Could these include living relatives of the dodo, unknown to the zoological world? Let us hope that other scientists will follow Mackal's lead, and investigate Tromelin and its islet neighbors. The zoological rewards could be high indeed.

The Last Mauritius Dodos?

The second item relating to recent survival of dodos actually concerns the Mauritius dodo itself, and provides tantalizing evidence that the species was alive after 1681. To my knowledge, I am the first person to document this in a cryptozoological publication.

Lawrence G. Green wrote a number of books dealing with his travels through Africa and the many remarkable, sometimes inexplicable, sights and reports that came his way there. His explorations and sojourns, however, were not limited to the African mainland, and in *Secret Africa* (1936) he devoted one chapter to a period of time that he spent on Mauritius. In it he had this to say:

> But is the dodo dead? I have looked upon the bones of the dodo in the museum at Port Louis, Mauritius, and I have heard the island people talk of the bird. Now these people living in the very home of the dodo never speak of it as extinct. They will tell you that the dodo has been seen many times since 1681.... They declare, in fact, that the dodo still lives in remote parts of the island, in inaccessible cliff caves and mountain forests.

The thought of dodos alive and well in modern-day Mauritius seems an incredible one, to say the least. So what are we to make of it? Is it tall tales on the part of the islanders or misidentification of some other species? Or, unthinkable to all but the most open-minded cryptozoologists, is it a simple statement of fact?

There is no doubt that Western explorers have been led astray on many occasions by fanciful tales told to them by the native inhabitants of a given area, and for a variety of different reasons. Sometimes there is a deliberate intention to deceive gullible Westerners. On other occasions, however, such tales have arisen out of sheer politeness on the part of the locals, agreeing with the Westerners and even encouraging their searches for bizarre beasts simply to please them. In addition, there is the ever-present problem of distinguishing between reality and native folklore. (The yeti saga is a case in point here.)

Yet in opposition to all of this is the undeniable fact that many native tales of seemingly impossible creatures have indeed resulted in the discovery of animals hitherto undescribed by modern science. The annals of cryptozoology are full of such animals—the okapi, gorilla, giant panda, kouprey, Congo peacock, onza, Vu Quang ox, and many others. Consequently, it is a foolhardy zoologist who as a matter of course dismisses native reports of mystery beasts as evidence for their existence.

With respect to the Mauritius dodo, then, let us not reject its post-1681 existence just yet. Is it in any way likely that "dodo" sightings were based on some other species that in some way resembles a dodo? The island of Samoa houses a huge pigeon known as the tooth-billed pigeon *Didunculus strigirostris*. Although it can fly, its combination of a powerful, notably hooked bill and its large portly build renders a surprisingly dodo-like appearance (hence *Didunculus*, "little dodo").

Indeed, the discovery and scientific description of this Samoan species in the mid-1800s provided supportive evidence that the dodos were themselves nothing more than oversized doves that had lost the ability to fly;

Samoa's dodo-like, tooth-billed pigeon.

until then, they had been variously classed as relations of vultures, cranes, and even, incredibly, short-legged ostriches!

As it happens, the tooth-billed pigeon is the only living species that in any way resembles a dodo. There is nothing else, either on Mauritius or elsewhere, that could be confused even for an instant with it. So we must pass over the misidentification possibility with regard to native reports of modern-day dodos, which thereby brings us to the third, and by far the most controversial, ostensibly inconceivable possibility. Namely, that dodos did indeed persist beyond 1681 and that, most fantastic of all, they may still be alive today.

In view of the longstanding popularity of Mauritius as a holiday retreat, it would seem impossible that such birds could exist without having been seen by non-natives. Yet we must recall that the habitats supposedly housing modern dodos are the very ones that holidaymakers and casual visitors to Mauritius would rarely if ever visit—mountain forests and inaccessible cliffs. Only native islanders would be aware of such localities and be in a position to pass through them. Even the island's original explorers scarcely frequented such areas, settling up settlements instead in the environmentally hospitable lowlands. Cryptozoologist Dr. Bernard Heuvelmans has pointed out that it is no accident that most reports of unknown terrestrial animals emerge from mountainous forests and other inaccessible, inhospitable regions.

Even so, we may be rash in ruling out entirely the lowlands of Mauritius when contemplating recent dodo survival. Speaking with his Mauritius-born wife and Mauritius friends, during the early 1990s cryptozoological explorer Bill Gibbons learned to his astonishment that on this island there is a secluded patch of rainforest called the Plain Champagne, stretching out to the coast where dodo-like birds have allegedly been seen in recent times at early dawn and dusk, walking upon the silent, half-lit beach. Folklore or fact? Gibbons is returning to Mauritius in July 1997 to investigate this remarkable claim, so we may not have to wait much longer for the answer.

It should go without saying that it is both impossible and illogical for anyone (scientist or otherwise) to claim that an animal cannot exist within a given area if that area has never been thoroughly explored. Such a person may just as well say that because he has never actually visited the Louvre in Paris himself, this museum cannot possibly house the Mona Lisa, and thereby dismiss the contrary evidence of innumerable eyewitnesses in exactly the same manner as science continues to ignore mystery beast reports originating from such creatures' human neighbors.

As dead as the dodo"—who knows? Perhaps a future exploration of Mauritius will find that the phrase, rather than its subject, is obsolete.

Ten

From Flying Toads to Snakes With Wings

British Monsters: Myth or Reality?

> *From ghoulies and ghosties and long-leggety beasties*
> *And things that go bump in the night,*
> *Good Lord, deliver us!*
>
> **—Scottish prayer**

To many people, the subject of British monsters is dominated by creatures such as sea serpents and their freshwater versions that may inhabit Loch Ness, not to mention a generous supply of pantheresque prowlers and other feline enigmas. Yet in reality, these are quite an insignificant percentage of the total spectrum of strange, often seemingly inexplicable mystery beasts on record from the United Kingdom. Some are certainly only myths and folktales, whereas others appear disconcertingly tangible. The trick, therefore, is to distinguish which are real, and which are not. However, this is not as easy a task to accomplish as it might seem. The following examples will all too readily demonstrate this truth.

Flying Toads and Snakes With Wings

One of the most formidable water monsters documented in John Rhys's exhaustive two-volume opus *Celtic Folk-Lore, Welsh and Manx* (1901) was the terrifying *llamhigyn y dwr* or water-leaper, which inhabited lonely stretches of river in Wales and devoured any hapless sheep or other livestock venturing into its freshwater domain. Its body's shape recalled that of a huge toad, but there the resemblance ended. Despite its name, the water-leaper lacked the toad's muscular, hopping hind legs. Instead, it had a tail—and a large pair of wings!

Nevertheless, this weird wonder did share one notable characteristic with the toad—a powerful voice, literally a hideous shriek, with which it deliberately frightened so thoroughly any unwary travelers seeking to cross the river that they would lose their footing and fall headlong into it. Once in the river, they would swiftly make a brief (and invariably fatal) acquaintance with its monstrous occupant. Happily, the loathsome llamhigyn y dwr does not appear to have been encountered lately.

In contrast, as recently as the first half of the nineteenth century an equally surprising Welsh mystery beast was met with so regularly that it was shot by farmers, who deemed it to be nothing more than vermin, of no greater significance than the rat or the fox. The principal setting for this extraordinary scenario was the expanse of woodland surrounding Penllyne Castle in Glamorgan, which according to recollections of various aged local

A gargoyle reminiscent of the dreaded *llamhigyn y dwr*.

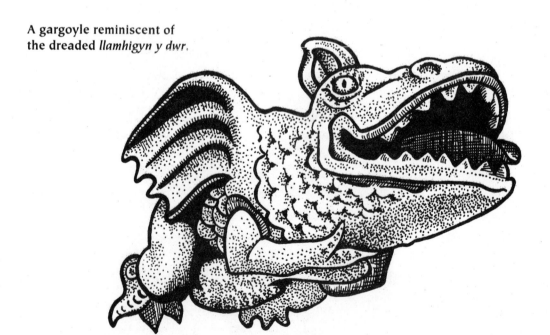

Winged serpents are impossible—aren't they?

people recorded by Marie Trevelyan in her book *Folk-Lore and Folk Stories of Wales* (1909), harbored a sizeable population of winged snakes.

Any type of snake with wings would be a zoological wonder, but the Penllyne variety was not ordinary even by these standards. Trevelyan documented the description given to her by an old man from Penllyne who remembered them well from his boyhood days. He said they were "...very beautiful." They were coiled when in repose, and "looked as if they were covered with jewels of all sorts. Some of them had crests sparkling with all the colours of the rainbow." When disturbed they glided swiftly, "sparkling all over," to their hiding places. When angry, they "flew over people's heads, with outspread wings bright, and sometimes with eyes too, like the feathers in a peacock's tail."

He said they were "no old story invented to frighten children," but a real fact. His father and uncle had killed some of them, for they were "as bad as foxes for poultry." The old man attributed the extinction of the winged serpents to the fact that they were "terrors in the farmyards and coverts."

Trevelyan also included the account of an elderly woman who, during her childhood, had spent some time in Penmark Place, Glamorgan, where such creatures were again a common sight in the nearby woods close to Porthkerry Park. The woman remembered her grandfather telling her that he and his brother had deliberately sought these winged snakes, and had succeeded in shooting one. It had attacked them after falling to the ground, but they eventually managed to kill it. She had seen its feathered skin, which her grandfather had kept until his death, and after which it was discarded.

The woman recalled that these strange creatures were infamous for their attacks on the local farmers' chickens. This provided independent corroboration for the statement to this effect made by the old man from Penllyne.

Needless to say, few zoologists would countenance the erstwhile existence of winged feathered serpents in Wales (or anywhere else), but what makes this particular case so difficult to dismiss is its troubling fusion of the flagrantly fantastic with the unutterably mundane. On one hand, there is a winged snake with a covering of feathers instead of scales—a zoological absurdity of the first order. Yet on the other hand, there is the extraordinary fact that its bizarre appearance was apparently of far less significance to the local populace than its irritating desire for their poultry. This is hardly the attitude one might expect in relation to a beast of legend or folklore. On the contrary, it mirrors the natural response of people so familiar with a real creature that its external wonder no longer attracts surprise or interest, especially when some mundane but annoying aspect of its behavior threatens their livelihood.

The slaughter of the remarkable tiger-striped thylacine (marsupial wolf) by Tasmanian sheep farmers during the early years of this century is a prime example of such a situation, and one whose tragic reality is only too familiar to conservationists and cryptozoologists alike.

Who knows? If the relatives of the Penmark woman's grandfather had not been so keen to discard his treasured specimen, the mystery of Glamorgan's winged serpents might be a mystery no longer.

The Blue Men of Minh and the Benebecula Mermaid

Difficulties in distinguishing myth from reality are not confined to winged serpents. The investigation of aquatic humanoids—the merfolk—can offer its fair share of surprises too.

Some British merfolk can readily be assigned to the realms of folklore. One example is the blue men of Minh, named after their blue skin and exclusive occurrence within the Minh strait separating the Hebridean islands of Shiant and Long. Although aggressive, they could be warded off by anyone with the verbal agility to address them solely in rhyme.

Belief in mermaids is as ancient as it is widespread.

Other merfolk, however, are much more problematic. Take, for instance, the Benbecula mermaid. This little-known case must surely be one of the most extraordinary of its kind on record. It was included in Vol. II of Alexander Carmichael's *Carmina Gadelica*, an invaluable four-volume encyclopedia of vanishing and vanished words, beliefs, and customs, collected orally by the author in Scotland's highlands and islands, and translated by him from Gaelic into English.

Carmichael recorded that around 1830, some people were cutting seaweed at Sgeir na Duchadh, in Grimnis, on the Outer Hebridean island of Benbecula, when one of the women saw a small woman-like creature splashing in the sea a few feet away. She called her companions, who came running to see this unexpected visitor somersaulting in the water.

The men in the group attempted to catch the creature, but it swam farther away, beyond their reach, until some of the boys accompanying the men threw stones at it. One struck the creature in the back, apparently scoring a fatal blow. A few days later its lifeless body was discovered washed ashore nearly two miles away, at Cuile in Nunton. Carmichael provided the following description of the corpse and its fate:

> The upper portion of the creature was about the size of a well-fed child of three or four years of age, with an abnormally developed breast. The hair was long, dark, and glossy, while the skin was white, soft, and tender. The lower part of the body was like a salmon, but without scales. Crowds of people, some from long distances, came to see this strange animal, and all were unanimous in the opinion that they had gazed on the mermaid at last.

> Mr. Duncan Shaw, factor for Clanranald, baron-bailie and sheriff of the district, ordered a coffin and shroud to be made for the mermaid. This was done, and the body was buried in the presence of many people, a short distance above the shore where it was found. There are persons still living who saw and touched this curious creature, and who give graphic descriptions of its appearance.

The most popular explanation for mermaids, as misidentified seals or seacows, may well apply to various reports of briefly spied sea creatures safely beyond reach and examination, but could it really be applicable in this particular case? Is it plausible that seafaring people like those of the Outer Hebrides, well acquainted with seals and other marine creatures, could genuinely be fooled by the dead body of any such animal into believing that they were looking at the corpse of a mermaid? It seems unlikely. After all, how many dead seals or whales have been ceremoniously laid to rest in a coffin and shroud, with a solemn crowd in attendance? Its body must have

Dr. Karl P. N. Shuker/Fortean Picture Library

Copenhagen's famous statue of "The Little Mermaid."

been decidedly humanoid to have elicited such a remarkable response. Seals and sea-cows may appear humanoid from a distance and in poor visibility, but they could hardly be misidentified when viewed as intimately as the Benbecula creature.

If the story of this mystifying entity is indeed true, then something very strange and possibly of immense cryptozoological importance was buried on that lonely Hebridean coastline more than 160 years ago. No doubt its remains have long since been washed away, reclaimed by the waves and returned to the undersea world from where it had emerged, all unsuspecting of its tragic fate, on that long-vanished day.

Let us hope that if any of its relatives do the same in the future, they will be treated more humanely by our own kind.

The Dobhar-Chú and the Dandy Hounds

Some "monsters" may be allied to animals already well known to science, but are of unexpected size or behavior.

Also called the master otter or king otter, according to Irish legend the *dobhar-chú* is an exceptionally large Irish otter attended by a vast number of

normal-sized specimens, but rarely seen by humans. A rare exception supposedly occurred once at Dhu-Hill, when such a creature was spied amid a
"court" containing about a hundred typical otters. Even the smallest portion of its predominently white pelt is deemed to be extremely valuable, as
it is said to prevent a horse from injury, a man from wounding by gunshot,
and a ship from being wrecked by the sea.

However, there is also a rather more sinister facet to the folklore of the
dobhar-chú. A traditional story still prevalent in parts of northwestern Ireland tells of how a young married woman called Grace Connolly was killed
by a dobhar-chú while bathing in County Leitrim's Glenade Lake near her
home. Her assassin was swiftly slain by her grief-stricken husband, but then
the dobhar-chú's own enraged mate emerged from the lake and pursued him
relentlessly, until he finally killed it.

This could be dismissed as a mere folktale, were it not for the fact that
Grace Connolly's grave does indeed exist in Congbháil (Conwall) Cemetery
in the townland of Drumáin (Drummans), forming part of the approach to
the Valley of Glenade from the coastal plain of north County Leitrim and
south County Donegal. On her gravestone (dated September 24, 1722) is a

Trevor Beer

Is the *dobhar-chú* a gigantic version of the otter?

carving that depicts the dobhar-chú itself—a recumbent animal with dog-like body and limbs, a long tail with tufted tip, unusually large paws, plus a long heavy neck and short head with tiny ears that are all like those of an otter. Moreover, as recently as May 1968, sightings of a mysterious beast closely resembling the creature sculpted on Grace Connolly's gravestone was seen by several eyewitnesses near Sraheens Lough. This is a lake on the island of Achill, located off the western coast of County Mayo, which is to the west of County Leitrim. Perhaps the dobhar-chú is more than just a myth after all. Who can say?

The weasel *Mustela nivalis* is typically a solitary hunter, but occasionally, usually during extremely severe winters when prey is scarce, several have been spied hunting together as a pack. (This can also occur with a large family of weasels prior to the cubs moving away to become independent adults.) These rare but dramatic sights have inspired a great deal of folklore, with parents warning their children to stay well away from such congregations, whose members became known as "dandy hounds" and were claimed to be extremely bloodthirsty.

Weasels hunting in packs are called dandy hounds.

Although weasel gangs are hardly likely to pose a serious threat to humans, it is reasonable to assume that starving weasels would be less timid and more desperate than well-fed specimens. Hence it may indeed be prudent, if you ever meet a dandy hound pack, to maintain a diplomatic distance from it, just in case!

Worth noting is that in Cornwall, dandy dogs are said to be satanic black dogs with horns and huge flaming eyes.

A Centaur, a Harpy, and a Satyr

The following trio seems more at home in classical Greek mythology than loose in the British countryside, which makes their apparent reality all the more difficult to explain.

A centaur of sorts was encountered in Ireland one spring evening in 1966, judging from the account given later to the press by one of its frightened eyewitnesses, Margaret Johnson, and included in Graham McEwan's *Mystery Animals of Britain and Ireland* (1986).

Accompanied by John Farrell, Johnson had been driving past the estate of Lord Dillon near Drogheda, in County Louth, when they were forced to brake sharply. In the road, just up ahead of them, stood an extremely large animal with a horse-like body. Looking out of the window, Johnson at first thought that the creature was indeed a horse—until it turned to look at her. Then she screamed in absolute horror, for she could see only too clearly that it had the face of a man!

And it was not an ordinary human face; instead, its eyes bulged grotesquely, its skin was hairy, and its mouth was grimacing in a hideous, evil leer. Petrified with fear, the two eyewitnesses were unable at first to flee from this horrific monstrosity, because for almost two minutes its enormous bulk continued to block their path, standing directly in front of their car upon its four sturdy, equine limbs. Then suddenly, just as abruptly as it had arrived, it vanished. The two shaken travelers drove rapidly away and on to Johnson's home, where they were so desperate to reach the safety of the house that they drove straight through the gate without even stopping to open it, sending it crashing off its hinges. For several days afterwards, Johnson remained extremely shaken and sick.

One of the most feared monsters of Irish mythology is the *pooka*, which often assumes the guise of a malevolent horse or pony. Is this what John Farrell and Margaret Johnson saw that night? But pookas are only imaginary, aren't they?

BUSINESS REPLY MAIL

FIRST-CLASS MAIL   PERMIT NO. 170   MARION, OHIO

POSTAGE WILL BE PAID BY ADDRESSEE

170 FUTURE WAY
PO BOX 1940
MARION, OH 43306-2040

PLACE
STAMP
HERE

FOR COURTESY REPLY ONLY

LLEWELLYN PUBLICATIONS
PO BOX 64383
SAINT PAUL MN 55164-0383

Amazingly, a very similar "semi-centaur" has also been reported from England. In February 1996, I appeared on a British ITV television show *This Morning* in a phone-in session concerning viewers' first-hand experiences of mystery animals. One of the callers was Nicky Knott, who claimed that while driving home along a back road in King's Lynn (near the Norfolk-Lincolnshire border) one evening a couple of years earlier, her husband saw what he initially thought was a horse or deer, standing at the right-hand side of the road. As he approached, however, he could plainly see that although it did have a horse's body and legs, its face was that of a man! Terrified, Knott drove on as fast as he could, leaving the monster far behind and not looking back once until he had reached home.

Equally macabre was a harpy-like horror known as the *skree*, which in 1746 was reputedly spied by no less eminent an eye-witness than Lord General Murray. This occurred when, just before the famous but disastrous battle of Culloden between the Duke of Cumberland's troops and the Jacobite rebels began in the Scottish Highlands, a monstrous winged beast with a human head and burning red eyes hovered on black leathery wings over a detachment of terrified soldiers, emitting spine-chilling shrieks like the very incarnation of death itself.

The skree has supposedly been spied on at least two further occasions. On May 22, 1915, during World War I, it reputedly appeared in the sky above a 500-strong group of Royal Scots men and officers about to catch a train at Larbert railway

Did a centaur like this appear in Ireland one evening in 1966?

The harpies of Greek mythology readily come to mind when contemplating the *skree* of Scotland.

station that would begin their journey to the Flanders fields. Alarmed by such an ill omen, the men had to be forced at gunpoint by their officers to mount the train. That train crashed later that same day and caught fire, killing 227 passengers and injuring 246 more.

In summer 1993, the skree was allegedly spied at a mist-shrouded rock outcrop by two lost hill walkers in Glencoe.

Not content with centaurs and harpies, Britain also has its own version of the classical satyr. Referred to as the *urisk*, it is described as half-man, half-goat. It supposedly inhabits the loneliest expanses of the Scottish Highlands, where it was sometimes venerated as a nature deity, rather like the Greek demi-god Pan, until the coming of Christianity.

Some authorities have suggested that the mysterious, seemingly malevolent entity reportedly inhabiting the lofty peak of Ben MacDhui in the Cairngorms and known as the Big Grey Man is a urisk. As reported in an article of mine (*FATE*, May 1990), over the years numerous climbers exploring this shadowy mountain have sensed the existence here of an unseen malign presence. Some experienced a sudden, all-consuming spasm of inexplicable panic that compelled them to flee from its peak as fast as they could run, occasionally sending them racing towards the very edge of its cliffs in their frantic bid to escape from the terror that they genuinely believed to be pursing them. Is it just a coincidence that, in its most literal sense, panic is the specific sensation of shock induced by the sudden presence of the satyr-like deity Pan?

Satyrs were half-man, half-goat, just like the *urisk*.

Fairy Hounds and Daisy Dogs

From the earliest times right up to the present day, people walking along certain lonely lanes in the U.K. have reported encountering huge phantasmal dogs—jet black in color, with glowing fiery eyes, sulfurous breath, and the ability to vanish into thin air—that bring certain death to anyone who touches them. Known as "black dogs," "devil dogs," and the "hounds of hell," these scary Baskervillian beasts are probably Britain's most well-known supernatural creatures, but they are not its only canine curiosities.

Equally eerie are the fairy hounds, but very different in outward form from the black dogs. Sometimes gracefully built, almost like deer, they have snow-white coats and distinctive red ears. Nevertheless, just as with the black dogs, the sudden appearance of one of these ethereal animals can be a portent of doom, especially if anyone should be unwise enough to touch it. Different again is Scotland's *cu sith*, the Highland fairy dog, distinguished from other canine entities by its dark green coat and its long tail, often curled up over its back.

Whereas those examples bear at least a superficial external similarity to corporeal dogs, the next two are instantly recognized as spectral in nature. The Gabriel hounds of Lancashire have the bodies of huge dogs, but human heads; the wish hounds of Dartmoor have no heads at all.

Yet perhaps the most remarkable canine specter of Britain is the daisy dog. As recounted in my book *Extraordinary Animals Worldwide* (1991), fishermen in Cornwall greatly fear meeting a small, silky-furred Pekingese-like dog, especially if they see it on a lonely stretch of coastline sitting near or upon a plot of earth bearing daisies in the shape of a cross.

Pekingese—
the key to the
Cornish daisy
dog mystery?

During the reign of Queen Elizabeth I, according to a centuries-old Cornish legend, the Emperor of China sent to England a pair of small, snub-faced dogs with silky coats and plume-like tails. These belonged to the greatly venerated Pekingese breed, and were to be a very special gift for the English monarch, together with a great quantity of gold.

They traveled by ship in the company of a Chinese princess, a mandarin, and many guardians and slaves; but by the time they had reached the last stage in their long and arduous journey, only the dogs, the princess, the mandarin, and a single slave remained alive. However, during that period the female Pekingese had given birth to a litter of puppies.

The dogs and their retinue were taken on board a Cornish fishing vessel, sailing to England, but the superstitious sailors became very alarmed by the silent, inscrutable princess, believing her to be a witch who would bring them disaster. Soon they killed her companions, and attempted to steal the gold, but were prevented by the dogs, who bit one of the sailors on his hand. In revenge, they threw the princess, the dogs, and the treasure overboard.

The princess' lifeless body drifted ashore, where it was found and buried by a simple but kind-hearted man. The waves also carried the dogs ashore, but except for the adult male these were all dead as well. So the man buried their tiny bodies alongside the princess'. Then he planted some daisies in the shape of the cross over their grave, and placed the little dog on top of the flowers as a guardian. After wagging his tail weakly and licking the man's hand, he died too. So the man walked home very sorrowfully, his eyes full of tears.

Word soon spread about the events aboard the Cornish vessel, and to everyone's additional horror the sailor who had been bitten by one of the Pekingeses died shortly afterwards—not from his injury, but from fear. The site of the grave consequently acquired the reputation of being an evil abode, and was shunned. Moreover, it is said that ever since the deaths of the princess and the dogs, their grave has been faithfully guarded by the spirit of the male Pekingese, who will not hesitate to bite anyone drawing too close or attempting to disturb the grave. To be bitten by this spectral creature, the daisy dog, is to meet certain death shortly afterwards. Even in modern times, some people claim to have seen it, resting atop the daisy-marked grave.

Perhaps the most remarkable aspect of this strange affair is that according to the accepted history of the breed, Pekingeses did not arrive in Britain until the late nineteenth century, when four were rescued from China's Summer Palace following the fall of the Manchu Dynasty. Thus an ancient Cornish legend accurately describes a distinctive breed of dog reaching

English shores more than 300 years *before* it officially first became known here. Clearly, there is still much to learn about the uncanny daisy dog.

The Cockatrice of Renwick

Many old churches have interesting histories, but few compare to that of the church at Renwick, a village in the northern English county of Cumbria. In 1733, during the demolition of an earlier version of the present-day church here, a monstrous black creature with huge bat-like wings emerged from its foundations. It was identified by onlookers as a cockatrice, a horrific winged serpent hatched by a toad from a shell-less egg laid by a cockerel. It was sporting its parents' characteristic wattles and coxcomb, and able to crow like a cockerel too.

Everyone ran home at once, to escape the wrath of this terrifying apparition—everyone, that is, except for a bold man called John Tallantine (spelled "Tallantire" in some accounts), who valiantly entered into combat with the monster in the churchyard. After a furious battle, Tallantine

The cockatrice—one of mythology's most feared beasts.

overcame his formidable assailant, slaying the cockatrice with a lance hewn from the rowan tree (which is famed for its magical combative properties against evil). In grateful thanks for his triumph in freeing the region from the creature, he and his descendants were ever afterwards granted exemption from paying tithes (a type of property-related tax).

A concise account of Renwick's history is kept in the current church at Renwick, and refers to the cockatrice episode. A copy of this account was very kindly supplied to me by the Reverend David Fowler, the vicar of the Benefice of Kirkoswald, Renwick and Ainstable; the relevant section reads as follows:

> The inhabitants of the Village are called "Renwick Bats" because they fled from a Cockatrice (Crack a Christ) monster flying out at them from the foundations of the old Church they were rebuilding in 1733. All fled except John Tallantine who armed with a Rowantree slew the monster. For this act his estate was enfranchised to him and his heirs forever.

How can such an amazing episode be explained? After all, whereas some fabulous animals were inspired by reports of real creatures later distorted in the retelling, it has been well established that the only basis in reality for the cockatrice is the curious but fully confirmed fact that occasionally hens will undergo a partial sex reversal, after which they develop the coxcomb of a cockerel, and sometimes gain the ability to crow like one. Yet such creatures can hardly account for the monster fought by Tallantine. So what was it that flew out from the church's foundations? No native British bat or bird is big enough or horrifying enough to be mistaken for a cockatrice. Once again, we have a case in which folklore and fact are so inextricably intertwined that it is impossible to separate them in our bid to uncover the identity of the mystery beast at its core.

The Cenaprugwirion: A Living Fossil in North Wales?

For a number of years, inhabitants in and around Abersoch in North Wales have reported sightings of a very strange type of large lizard, locally termed the *cenaprugwirion*, *genaprugwirion*, or daft flycatcher. Apparently, there used to be a notable population of this creature, but it has become rare lately.

According to eyewitnesses, it is about one foot long and mud-brown in color, with a head the size of an orange, very mobile eyes, a large tongue that it uses for catching flies, and a prominent dewlap (flap of skin beneath its chin). It inhabits burrows in the ground or in earthen banks.

This description does not match any native British reptile, and since learning about the cenaprugwirion I have consulted several herpetologists for their opinions as to what it could be. All agree that it must be a foreign species that has escaped from captivity and has established itself in this area, just like so many other non-native species elsewhere in Britain, including such exotica as wallabies, porcupines, and parakeets. The identities on offer vary, from iguanas to chameleons, but one in particular is of great interest: the tuatara *Sphenodon punctatus*.

Although superficially lizard-like, this native of New Zealand is famed as the only living genus of a totally separate lineage of reptiles, the sphenodontids, which were contemporary with the dinosaurs but died out with them—except for the line leading to the tuatara. It survived in New Zealand because the land mass comprising this dual-island country contained no native mammals that could compete with it.

Are New Zealand's tuatara and Wales' *cenaprugwirion* one and the same species?

Tragically, however, once Westerners reached New Zealand and began introducing Western predatory mammals such as cats, dogs, and rats, the tuatara's numbers rapidly fell. Today it exists only on a few offshore islets and in captivity, having been extirpated on the North and South Islands. (A second, smaller species, *S. guntheri*, is wholly confined to tiny North Brother Island.)

Nevertheless, during the nineteenth century when it was still relatively common, it was frequently exported to many Western countries for zoos and private collections. Although highly unlikely, it is not impossible that some could have escaped and survived in the British countryside (tuataras have an extremely long life span), eventually establishing viable populations. Certainly, the tuatara does bear a surprising similarity to the description of the mysterious cenaprugwirion, and also shares its preference for inhabiting burrows and its ability to survive at temperatures as low as those prevalent during British winters. So what is the answer? Is it just an example of droll Welsh whimsy, or a creature of cryptozoological significance?

How ironic but marvelous it would be if investigations revealed that, after being virtually exterminated in its native homeland, one of the world's most famous species of "living fossil" had been successfully thriving in scientific anonymity for the past century or so many thousands of miles away in rural North Wales!

The modern world's potential for offering cryptozoological surprises is not exhausted, even in a land as supposedly well explored zoologically as Britain. We may not uncover an okapi or a coelacanth here, but who knows what its deceptively uncontroversial countryside could unfurl in future years? From flying toads to snakes with wings? Watch this space!

Eleven

The Quest for the *Real* Golden Fleece

Was Jason's Voyage More than Just a Yarn?

This rising Greece with indignation viewed,
And youthful Jason an attempt conceived
Lofty and bold: along Pene´us' banks,
Around Olympus' brows, the Muses' haunts,
He roused the brave to re-demand the fleece.

—John Dyer
The Fleece, ii

One of the most famous episodes in Greek mythology concerns the quest by the hero Jason and his loyal band of Argonauts for the fabulous Golden Fleece. This fleece was derived from a magical winged ram called Chrysomallus, sent to earth by the messenger god Hermes. A charming tale, but indisputably fictional—or is it? Could the Golden Fleece be more than a legend?

Surprisingly, science—so frequently the annihilator of folklore and fancy—actually provides evidence for believing that Jason's shimmering quarry may have had a factual basis.

Was the Fleece Used to Trap Gold?

As far back as the first century B.C., the Greek geographer Strabo had contemplated the possibility that the Golden Fleece legend was founded in reality. He suggested that it may have been an ordinary fleece that had been used to trap gold washed down

Martin Cannon

Jason, Medea, and the fabulous golden fleece of the winged ram Chrysomallus.

the River Phasis. Particles of gold would have remained ensnared among its fibers, resulting in a fleece that at least on casual observation might well have appeared to be composed of gold-bearing wool.

Although a most ingenious idea, it is surely unlikely that such a superficially deceptive artifact could not only have retained its illusion intact during inevitable closer examination, but also have become sufficiently famous to engender one of Greek mythology's most enduring legends.

In his informative work *The Subterranean World* (third edition, 1875), Dr. George Hartwig did point out that even today sheep fleeces are still used to trap particles of gold in rivers by natives of gold-possessing countries. How-ever, he also noted that this was not taken by many authorities as proof that the Golden Fleece was itself a fleece with gold-ensnared fibers. On the con-trary, many felt that the quest by Jason and company was not for a Golden Fleece at all, but for the gold itself, with the fleece being nothing more than a means of obtaining the gold and having no significance of its own.

In short, the Golden Fleece's present-day prominence in mythology might be due to erroneous telling and retelling of the ancient myths down through the ages, with the object of Jason's quest (the gold) becoming confused with the means of obtaining it (an ordinary sheep fleece).

Was It a Fine-Wooled Fleece?

Another solution, offered by several different researchers, is one that seeks to explain the Golden Fleece in a totally separate manner, as a misinter-preted and/or mythified reference to fine-wooled fleeces. There are three principal classes of wool:

1. Carpet wool (very coarse and hair-like; used for making carpets and rugs).

2. Cross-bred wool (familiar, weaving-quality; produced by the majority of British sheep breeds).

3. Fine wool (valuable and lustrous, with exceedingly fine fibers lacking a central medulla; generally obtained today from Merino sheep).

In a paper published by *Nature* on April 13, 1973, Drs. M. L. Ryder and J. W. Hedges from Edinburgh's ARC Animal Breeding Research Organiza-tion noted that fine-wooled sheep were certainly known in antiquity. Additionally, they announced that specimens of Scythian fine wool exam-ined by them and derived from the Black Sea area demonstrated that sheep yielding such wool existed as far back as the fifth century B.C. This is particularly significant, because as Ryder and Hedges noted, not only has the Golden Fleece legend been taken by some researchers to refer to fine wool, but in addition it is of similar date and is associated with the same area as the Scythian wool discussed by them in their paper. This newly found correspondence therefore adds credence to the postulated link between the Golden Fleece and fine wool.

Merino sheep—a famous breed of fine-wooled sheep.

Nonetheless, in 1932 a paper had already appeared in the *Proceedings of the Royal Society* (London) that was destined in the 1980s to suggest a much more literal solution to the Golden Fleece mystery than a gold-bearing artifact, a substitute for gold itself, or a mythification of early fine-wooled sheep.

Was the Gold From *Within* the Sheep?

The paper in question was written by Drs. Claude Rimington and A. M. Stewart of the Wool Industries Research Association of Leeds, Yorkshire, and concerned itself with a previously uninvestigated pigment. Raw wool comprises the wool fibers and "yolk." This latter component in turn consists of ether-soluble grease (secreted by the sheep's sebaceous skin glands) and a water-soluble substance known as suint (secreted by the sheep's sweat glands). In their paper, Rimington and Stewart recorded that a golden brown coloration existed in varying intensities within the suint of certain sheep. Its intensity of color depended on the animals' diet and age, and was influenced by conditions stimulating sweat.

Following their analysis of the composition and secretion of this mysterious pigment (which they termed lanaurin, meaning "golden wool"),

Rimington and Stewart concluded that it was a pyrrolic complex—a compound whose chemical structure is based on a ring of four carbon atoms and one nitrogen atom. Moreover, they believed it to be related to the bile pigment bilirubin—a reddish substance originating via the breakdown of the well-known respiratory pigment hemoglobin, and normally secreted into the bile by the liver in many mammalian species.

Rimington and Stewart suggested that the appearance of lanaurin resulted from an enhanced destruction of hemoglobin within the sheep so afflicted; they also confirmed that it was conveyed through the skin of such sheep into their wool via the sweat glands. Furthermore, not only did this compound occur within the wool of golden-colored sheep, it was also found within their urine, which in turn was excessively pigmented. Comparisons were drawn between golden-wooled sheep and inherited acholuric jaundice in humans, with the suggestion that as with this type of human jaundice, the golden-wool condition in sheep may be genetically based.

Further research into this intriguing area of biochemistry took place in the years to come. Chemical analyses became more precise, and chemical nomenclature diversified; substances inducing jaundice became known as icterogenic agents. By the early 1960s, examples of abnormal golden coloration had been reported and studied not only in sheep but also in rabbits (see the series of papers by Rimington and colleagues published during this period in the Royal Society's *Proceedings*). It emerged that a number of natural and synthetic icterogenic agents belonged to a group of chemicals known as the pentacyclic triterpenoids. In other words, they are organic compounds produced in animals and also plants by combination (into larger molecules) of units each containing five carbon atoms arranged in the characteristic pattern present in isoprene (a simple-structured substance used in the manufacture of rubber).

By 1963 and in partnership with J. M. M. Brown and Barbara Sawyer, Rimington's continuing research in this field had uncovered some important new information. They revealed that the golden-wool condition in sheep could also be induced by environmental means, namely, the ingestion by sheep of leaves from certain plants (especially shrubs of the genus *Lantana*). These plants contained pentacyclic triterpenoids that poisoned the liver of such sheep, thus preventing the normal excretion of bilirubin into the bile. Instead, it passed (together with various related pigments) into the skin and wool suint of those animals, thereby bestowing upon their wool the golden appearance reported in Rimington's earlier studies.

So here we have an environmentally stimulated phenomenon that produces sheep (and rabbits) with golden colored wool.

Not surprisingly, therefore, it was only a matter of time before this circumstance was mooted as the solution to the fabled Golden Fleece itself. In a letter to *Nature* published on June 23, 1987, this was indeed proposed in that context by Dr. G. J. Smith, a researcher in physical chemistry at Melbourne University in Australia. In his letter, Dr. Smith recalled an earlier portion of the Golden Fleece legend. Namely, the section in which its ovine bearer appeared during a period of severe famine in Greece, having been sent by Hermes to rescue two children due to be sacrificed by their evil stepmother Ino, in an attempt to appease the gods and thereby end the famine.

Smith noted that during modern-day periods of famine in New Zealand, sheep were often fed leaves from trees by their distraught farmer owners. He then postulated that under similar conditions in Greece, farmers may well have fed their sheep leaves from the extensively cultivated olive tree *Olea europea*. It just so happens that the olive tree's leaves contain great amounts of oleanolic acid, which is the basic substance from which the known icterogenic pentacyclic triterpenoids are derived.

When fed to sheep, the leaves of olive trees could produce golden wool.

Tests carried out with rabbits by Brown, Rimington, and Sawyer in the 1960s had readily revealed that small amounts of oleanolic acid did not induce any icterogenic activity. Conversely, as argued by Smith, when present in much greater concentrations, as in the leaves of the olive tree (and particularly in those subjected to draught stress, as experienced in famine conditions)—oleanolic acid could exert a deleterious effect on the liver of sheep, and in turn bring about abnormal golden discoloration of wool. In short, the Golden Fleece legend may have been based on sightings of sheep that, during the famine periods experienced by Greece in earlier days, had fed on olive tree leaves, whose high triterpenoid content had ultimately caused their fleeces to be stained with golden bile pigments.

Although, as Smith himself admitted, this is all speculative, there is no doubt that it offers an exceedingly beguiling solution to the legend. It is a solution, moreover, that actually corresponds very closely not just with its principal but also with its more peripheral portions.

At the same time, however, some contrary evidence also exists, as brought to attention in a follow-up letter to *Nature* (published on November 5, 1987) by research chemists Drs. Patrick Moyna and Horacio Heinzen from Uruguay's Universidad de la Republica. They reported that oleanolic acid is contained in even greater concentrations in certain other plant sources; for example, it accounts for up to 50 percent of the content of grapes' epicuticular wax. Yet this does not appear to have any toxic effect on humans consuming the grapes. This is in contrast to the outcome that one would have predicted, judging from the arguments offered with sheep and olive leaves. However, Moyna and Heinzen did not provide any references in relation to sheep and grapes, and it is well known that the gastrointestinal tract and its associated organs in humans differ very considerably in morphology and physiology from those of sheep. Consequently, the matter remains unresolved with regard to these animals.

For the present, therefore, some very persuasive arguments exist in favor of a literal reality for the Golden Fleece, even if the concept of a starving, liver-damaged sheep with wool discolored by bile pigments does not arouse quite the same degree of romance and mystery as the lustrous, glittering Golden Fleece of mythology's magical ram. An unexpected source of support, perhaps, for Shakespeare's famous line: "All that glisters is not gold"?

Ultimately, however, it seems most unlikely that the Fleece's legend can ever become anything more than a subject for speculation. Did Jason's golden-hued quarry really exist, or was it (literally) nothing more than a yarn?

Twelve

In the Wake of Mystery Whales

Seeking Mighty Monsters of the Deep

The whale, the whale! Up helm, up helm! Oh, all ye sweet powers of air, now hug me close! Let not Starbuck die, if die he must, in a woman's fainting fit. Up helm, I say—ye fools, the jaw! the jaw! Is this the end of all my bursting prayers? all my life-long fidelities? Oh, Ahab, Ahab, lo, thy work. Steady! helmsman, steady. Nay, nay! Up helm again! He turns to meet us! Oh, his unappeasable brow drives on towards one, whose duty tells him he cannot depart. My God, stand by me now!

—Herman Melville
Moby Dick

Scientifically speaking, only the most infinitesimal proportion of our world's immense oceans and seas can be said to be well known. Yet for much of this century, remarkably few zoologists have been willing to consider seriously that they could offer up sizeable creatures of a form wholly unknown (at least in the living state) to science. This is in itself a very anomalous attitude, but what makes it even more so is that it persists even in the face of an ever-increasing list of major new species of aquatic animal discovered since 1900 (as already surveyed in Chapter 1, and comprehensively reviewed in my book *The Lost Ark: New and Rediscovered Animals of the 20th Century*, 1993).

These zoological debutantes include a rich diversity of cetaceans—those water-dwelling mammals comprising the baleen (toothless) whales, beaked whales, sperm whales, narwhal, porpoises, killer whales, and a heterogeneous assemblage of marine and freshwater species all loosely termed dolphins. Since 1900, the existence of at least thirteen new species of cetacean has been formally documented: two porpoises, one killer whale, one marine dolphin, one river dolphin, and eight beaked whales. The latest is Bahamonde's beaked whale *Mesoplodon bahamondi*, which first came to attention when a skull from a hitherto unknown species was found recently on Robinson Crusoe Island, Chile. It was formally described in 1996, but may not be the last new cetacean to be unveiled during the twentieth century. Numerous documented reports exist that describe sightings (often made by excellent eyewitnesses) of mysterious forms radically different from all cetacean species presently known to science.

Rhinoceros Dolphin and Rhinoceros Whale

Take, for example, the so-called rhinoceros dolphin—a mystifying creature measuring about nine feet long and with distinctive black-and-white markings, but named after the alleged presence of an extra dorsal fin, borne upon its head, and curving backwards like a rhino's horn. This bizarre beast could readily be dismissed as fantasy, were it not for its notable list of eyewitnesses.

The most important sighting on record was made by Jean Quoy and Joseph Gaimard, leaders of the *Uranie* and *Physicienne* expedition, who observed an entire school of these strange dolphins in the Pacific Ocean, while sailing between the Hawaiian Islands and New South Wales in October 1819. In Louis de Freycinet's *Voyage Autour du Monde...* (1824), they named it *Delphinus rhinoceros*, unaware that this form had already been christened *Oxypterus mongitori* by naturalist Constantin-Samuel Rafinesque-Schmalz in 1814. He based his description of it on a sighting by Antonio Mongitore of a specimen stranded on the Sicilian coast in

The perplexing rhinoceros dolphin.

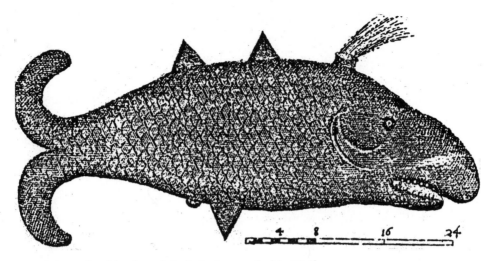

Mongitore's double-dorsal "whale," stranded in Sicily.

September 1741. However, as noted by Michel Raynal and Jean-Pierre Sylvestre (*Aquatic Mammals*, 1991), Mongitore's specimen bore litle resemblance to those of Quoy and Gaimard. Indeed, it may not even have been a cetacean at all, but merely a very large shark.

Also worth noting is that whereas the fins of fishes normally contain skeletal components, in cetaceans the dorsal fin is nothing more than a mass of connective tissue. Morphologically, therefore, the presence of an additional dorsal fin on a cetacean's head is actually rather less startling (and rather more plausible) than one might otherwise imagine it to be.

Although the rhinoceros dolphin's reality remains unproven, its history is fairly well known to cetological and cryptozoological researchers. In contrast, very few have ever heard of the rhinoceros whale. This is particularly tragic, for unlike most cryptozoological cetaceans, which seemingly belong to the suborder of odontocete (toothed) whales, the rhinoceros whale is apparently a mysticete (baleen) whale.

The principal record for this obscure creature is a sighting made by Italian naturalist Professor Enrico Giglioli on September 4, 1867, off the coast of Chile in the southeastern Pacific, while he was voyaging around the world on the steamer *Magenta*. According to his description, it resembled a baleen whale (tellingly, its mouth contained black whalebone). It was approximately sixty feet long, with a greenish gray back, grayish-white underparts, long falciform flippers, and two well-developed, erect dorsal fins. Both of these were triangular and were separated from one another by a large, apparently smooth space measuring about six and a half feet in length. During Giglioli's sighting, the whale blew several times, on the first occasion emitting a very noisy, resonant spout.

In 1870, Giglioli formally documented his double-dorsal sea beast, which he named *Amphiptera pacifica*. Moreover, as revealed by Raynal and Sylvestre, other reports of what may have been this same cryptic species were logged from Stonehaven, Scotland, in October 1898 by Alexander Taylor and crew on their fishing boat, *Lily*; and from the Mediterranean on July 17, 1983, by the crew of a sailboat traveling between Corsica and Cavalaire, France, whose boat was reputedly followed by one of these animals.

High-Finned Mystery Whales

Equally perplexing are certain mysterious forms of whales with an extremely high dorsal fin, and which have been reported from many different localities around the world.

One of these—forty-five to sixty feet long and with teeth only in the lower jaw—resembles a sperm whale, except for its dorsal fin and more rounded head. Two stranded specimens were recorded near the Shetland Islands in 1692 by cetological pioneer Sir Robert Sibbald, who dubbed their still-unrecognized species *Physeter tursio*, and likened their dorsal fin to a mizzen mast.

Another high-finned form, whose dorsal fin was at least five feet in length and stood erect upon the highest part of its back, was a grayish black whale roughly twenty-five feet long viewed on April 7, 1868, by E. W. H. Holdsworth, a fellow of London's Zoological Society, while he was becalmed a few miles off Chilaw on Sri Lanka's western coast. Reporting this animal in the society's *Proceedings* for 1872, he said that he was convinced it was not a killer whale, the only known species with a dorsal fin recalling his cetacean's. Holdsworth learned from some of his vessel's crew that it was a familiar creature to them, which they termed the "Palmyra fish." (Presumably the whale's tall erect fin reminded them of the palmyra, a tree prevalent in their native Malabar home.) They also stated that it was most often spied to the west of Cape Comorin, west of Sri Lanka, at India's southern tip.

Back in 1841, yet another version, black in color and this time with the erect dorsal fin sited farther back on its body, had been seen by Captain Sir James C. Ross near Antarctica's Ross Island, as recorded by him six years

Sperm whales lack the high dorsal reported by Sir Robert Sibbald for his Shetland mystery whale.

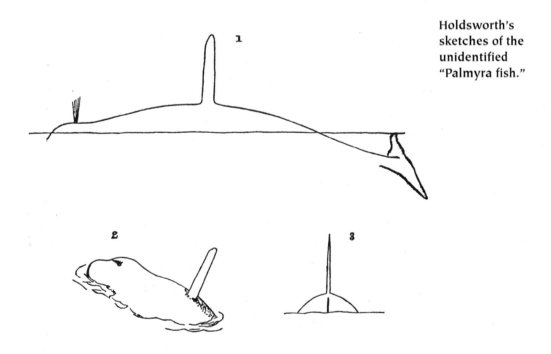

Holdsworth's sketches of the unidentified "Palmyra fish."

later in *A Voyage of Discovery and Research in the Southern and Antarctic Regions, During the Years 1839–43* (Vol. 1). It was also sighted by Dr. Edward Wilson, on both January 28 and February 8, 1902, while participating in Scott's *Discovery* expedition. More than sixty years later, on November 24 and November 27, 1964, eight sightings of some comparable whales were recorded by cetologist Dr. Robert Clarke and colleagues during a whale-marking and observation cruise off the Chilean coast.

Also noteworthy is the "monster" that spouted like a whale, bore a high dorsal fin, and was seen at Digby, Nova Scotia, on August 27, 1946. Interestingly, as reported in *Doubt* (No. 16), fishermen who observed it called it a "black fish," a name sometimes colloquially applied to the sperm whale.

Scrag Whale: A Rough-Backed Riddle of the Seas?

Other than the rhinoceros whale, the only controversial cetacean that seems to be a baleen form is the scrag whale *Balaena gibbosa*. In the *Philosophical Transactions* for 1725, it was described by the Hon. Paul Dudley, an English naturalist, as "Nearly akin to the Fin-back, but instead of a fin upon its back, the ridge of the after-part of its back is scragged with half a dozen knobs or knuckles."

This enigmatic creature was subsequently accorded a variety of different identities, including a mutilated rorqual (fin-back) and an immature right whale. In reality, however, it now appears that the scrag whale was a rare Atlantic version of the Pacific gray whale *Eschrichtius robustus*. Regrettably, it is now certainly extinct. Indeed, as long ago as the mid-1800s whalers had already ceased to report sightings of this distinctive cetacean.

Unidentified Dolphins and Beaked Whales

In his *Field Guide of Whales and Dolphins* (1971), Captain Willem Mörzer Bruyns records a number of seemingly unknown dolphins. Among these are a Senegalese form most comparable to the bridled dolphin *Stenella attenuata*, which he sighted in considerable numbers, and a Mediterranean version (the "Greek dolphin") reminiscent of the striped dolphin *S. coeruleoalba* in outline but lacking its diagnostic body markings. He also lists the so-called Illigan dolphin, a pink-bellied, yellow-flanked form that resembles in shape and size the melonhead whale *Peponocephala electra*, an

Thirteen

More Precious than Diamonds?

A Rose-Horned, Snow-Furred, Claw-footed Controversy

There ain't no such animal.

—**New Jersey farmer seeing dromedary at circus,
from a cartoon in *Life* (November 7, 1907)**

Mystery beasts come in all shapes and sizes, and are famous, if not infamous, for appearing in the most unlikely places.

So too are documented reports of them. Take the following example—one of the most extraordinary and mystifying that I have encountered, but one that had not previously been brought to cryptozoological attention.

The Abbé Emanuel Domenech's *Missionary Adventures in Texas and Mexico: A Personal Narrative of Six Years' Sojourn in Those Regions*, published in 1858, may not seem on first sight to be the type of book to hold much promise for seekers of unknown animals. Yet how wrong first appearances can be.

Tucked away inside this unassuming little volume, on pages 122–123, to be precise, is a truly remarkable report of an equally remarkable creature. According to Domenech, an American officer assured him that at Fredericksburg, Texas, he had seen a Comanche Indian woman who was:

...always accompanied by a very singular animal about the size of a cat, but of the form and appearance of a goat. Its horns were rose-coloured, its fur was of the finest quality, glossy like silk and white as snow; but instead of hoofs this little animal had claws. This officer offered five hundred francs for it; and the commandant's wife, who also spoke of this animal, offered a brilliant [diamond] of great value in exchange for it; but the Indian woman refused both these offers, and kept her animal, saying that she knew a wood where they were found in abundance; and promised, that if she ever returned again, she would catch others expressly for them.

Needless to say, in best mystery beast tradition, not only did the Indian woman never return, but the origin and nature of her enigmatic pet were

Is this what the Comanche woman's claw-footed pseudo-goat looked like?

never discovered either. Nothing more at all seems to have been recorded in relation to this most curious creature—a claw-footed pseudo-goat, for want of a better name—that bears no resemblance to any known animal, living or extinct.

The possession of horns suggests that it might have been some type of ungulate or hoofed mammal, the mammalian group containing the greatest number of horned species. Yet, paradoxically, its feet were not hoofed but clawed. True, there was once a group of horse-related ungulates known as chalicotheres, which, unlike most other ungulates, did indeed possess claws rather than hooves, but these were all relatively large, hornless species. They are believed to have died out entirely by the close of the Pleistocene epoch, around 10,000 years ago, and North America's representatives had in any case become extinct much earlier than that. So too had all other New World, clawed ungulates, which included certain notoungulates such as *Protypotherium* (an interatheriid) and *Homalodotherium*, both from Argentina's Miocene epoch, ending around five million years ago.

If the unrecognized species represented by the Comanche's pet was truly as common as she had inferred, it is unlikely that it would remain wholly unknown to science more than a century after the Abbé Domenech's report. Unlikely, but not impossible; it must be remembered that accounts of a cheetah-like Mexican mystery cat termed the onza by Sonoran inhabitants were dismissed as fantasy for more than three centuries, until on January 1, 1986, an onza was shot, and its body made available for full examination by a team of scientists, including J. Richard Greenwell, secretary of the International Society of Cryptozoology (see Chapter 1).

The reality of the onza can no longer be denied, so perhaps after more than a century it is still not too late to pursue the trail of the rose-horned, snow-furred, claw-footed controversy documented in the Abbé Domenech's book. The American writer John Burroughs once said: "There is always a new page to be turned in natural history if one is sufficiently on the alert." In the case of the cryptic creature discussed here, it is possible that a previously overlooked page from the past may yet lead to the writing of a most important new chapter in the future.

Certainly, if there are any readers with a knowledge of Domenech's life and travels, they would be well advised to follow whatever clues may still exist regarding the Texan locality likely to have been the original home of the Comanche woman's pseudo-goat. Who knows? Their investigations may well uncover nothing—or they could lead to a major zoological discovery.

Fourteen

When Tessie Met Teggie...

Lesser-Known Lake Monsters from Around the World

In England there were originally vast plains where the plentiful supply of water could gather. The streams were deep and slow, and there were holes of abysmal depth, where any kind and size of antediluvian monster could find a habitat. In places, which now we can see from our windows, were mudholes a hundred or more feet deep. Who can tell us when the age of the monsters which flourished in slime came to an end? There must have been places and conditions which made for greater longevity, greater size, greater strength than was usual. ...The lair of such a monster would not have been disturbed for hundreds—or thousands—of years. Moreover, these creatures must have occupied places quite inaccessible to man. ...Far be it from me to say that in more elemental times such things could not have been.

—Bram Stoker
The Lair of the White Worm

It is possible that many freshwater lakes around the world contain large animal forms unknown to science (at least in the living state). This fascinating subject shows no sign of waning. To date, however, interest has largely focused on just a small number of cases—Nessie of Scotland's Loch Ness, Champ of the U.S.A.'s Lake Champlain, Ogopogo of Canada's Lake Okanagan, the *mokele-mbembe* of the Congo's Lake Tele. The great majority of other "monster" lakes attract far less public attention. In order to rectify this situation, here is a round-up of news from a wide-ranging selection of these lesser-known monster lakes.

Memphré: Water Dragon of Quebec

We begin with North America's Lake Memphremagog, straddling the Quebec-Vermont border, and its monster-in-residence, Memphré. Thanks to interest in the latter, the study of lake monsters received a highly novel, semi-official name.

A plesiosaur (life-size model), a popular identity for some lake monsters.

Since 1978, former insurance broker Jacques Boisvert from Magog, Quebec, has been collecting reports of Memphré, some dating back to the early nineteenth century. By the middle of 1988, he had made well over 2,000 scuba-diving forays of this thirty-two-mile-long lake in search of its alleged inhabitant. One of Boisvert's friends, a monk at the St. Benoit du Lac Benedictine Abbey on Lake Memphremagog's shores, suggested that in view of the nature of his new occupation, Boisvert should call himself a dracontologist—literally, a dragon studier.

In June 1986, Boisvert and Barbara Malloy—a lady from Newport, Vermont, with a similar interest in Memphré—formed the International Society of Dracontology of Lake Memphremagog, and just a few months later the subject received major front-page coverage in the *Boston Globe*. Then, as reported in the *ISC Newsletter* for summer 1987, the Memphré movement subsequently gathered sufficient momentum for Vermont legislators to adopt on March 17, 1987, a joint resolution by the Senate and House of Representatives, requesting serious scientific investigation and formal protection of the Lake Memphremagog monster. Five years earlier, a similar resolution had been passed in relation to Champ of Lake Champlain by the legislative bodies of New York and Vermont.

But what of Memphré itself? What does this mystery beast (or beasts) look like? According to reports gathered by Boisvert that involved clear sightings, it resembles a long-necked, dragon-headed creature that moves at a steady pace through the water, almost as if propelled mechanically. Other accounts merely describe a Nessie-type hump.

On August 7, 1992, a six-foot-long hump, shiny brown-green and about as wide as the top of a Volkswagon Beetle, was spied at a distance of roughly 200 feet by science teacher Edward Lilly, his wife, and their nephew and niece while traveling on the lake in a boat. The hump was preceded by a sizeable wake, and rose about two feet above the water surface, undulating up and down, but remaining visible for thirty-five to forty seconds before heading away due north towards the Canadian border.

In an interview published by Montreal's *Gazette* on August 27, 1988, Boisvert recalled that the world-famous German scuba diver Max Leubker searched the lake back in 1935. He had been hired by a wealthy family to locate the body of one of its members, which had never resurfaced after the person in question had drowned there earlier that year. Despite descending more than 200 feet into the lake (a depth that few divers can attain), Leubker never found the body, but did report seeing some very large eels "6–8 feet long and as thick as a man's thigh...," creatures that not even Boisvert himself had seen during his own dives in more recent years.

British Columbia's Lake Shuswap Monster: Mammal or Snake?

Another elongate Canadian monster may inhabit Lake Shuswap, in central British Columbia. While sailing on the lake on June 3, 1984, Linda Griffiths observed a patch of water 300 feet away that began to churn violently. Focusing on the area with binoculars, she perceived seven hump-like objects, grayish brown in color, visible above the water surface and moving in a straight line at a rapid pace. Mrs. Griffiths said that it resembled a fast-moving snake, twenty to twenty-five feet in total length.

Her two children (ages twelve and fifteen) and a friend of theirs (age thirteen) also saw it, and without binoculars, but none could distinguish any definite head. It crossed in front of the boat before finally submerging (*ISC Newsletter*, spring 1986). It is unlikely to have been a snake, as these normally swim via lateral undulations rather than vertical ones, but mammals and eels can create vertical disturbances.

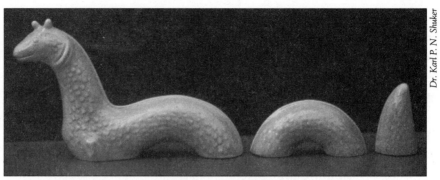

Perhaps this is what the monster of Lake Shuswap looks like.

Are These Monsters Ancient Whales?

As discussed within my book *In Search of Prehistoric Survivors* (1995), a popular identity for many lake monsters is a surviving species of zeuglodont—"officially" extinct for 25 million years. These were specialized whales with very elongated, almost serpentine bodies. Some were comparable in length to the object reported by Griffiths, and they had a well-delineated neck (unlike modern-day whales) so they could raise their head. A zeuglodont, therefore, might be expected to yield a similar outline to that of the Lake Shuswap monster (popularly referred to as Shuswaggi), and its head could perhaps be mistaken for one of the humps resulting from vertical undulations of its elongated body when swimming.

Skeleton and reconstruction of a zeuglodont.

to be deadly poisonous and capable of preying on creatures as large as medium-sized birds and rodents. Science has yet to examine a sapo de loma, but as I pointed out in my book *The Lost Ark: New and Rediscovered Animals of the 20th Century* (1993), the world's longest species of toad, the Colombian giant toad *Bufo blombergi*, was first made known to science as recently as 1951. So perhaps even larger species do still exist in remote regions of the world.

European Lake Monsters

In November 1995, a team of government-supported investigators journeyed to Turkey's largest lake, Lake Van, in search of a dinosaur-like beast reported here by several eyewitnesses. These include Bestami Alkan, Van Province's deputy governor, who spotted the monster six months earlier when picknicking here. Another prominent observer is Zeki Ergezen, the MP for Bitlis Province, who claims to have seen it while visiting the lake with his wife.

According to some accounts, the Lake Van monster is black in color, approximately twenty-four to thirty feet long, with triangular spines on its back (possibly a series of erect fins?), and a very hairy, horned head (but is its "hair" a true mane, or simply hair-like filaments?). Other descriptions, conversely, portray it as a white monster, with a black stripe on its back. There are even reports of two monsters seen together, which would presumably explain the two very different descriptions of the beast cited here.

To confuse matters even further, a monster has also been reported from Lake Ercek, about twelve miles east of Lake Van, which eyewitnesses have likened to a white aquatic horse.

The former Soviet Union's answer to Nessie and Champ is the monster of Lake Kok-Kol, situated in the Dzambul area of Kazakhstan. Said to have a body measuring up to fifty feet in total length, and a head exceeding six feet, it had attracted great interest from Soviet scientists during the 1970s and early 1980s. By 1986, however, expeditions in search of it had come up with an identity rejecting any lake monster considerations.

One of the creature's most distinctive attributes was its frequently reported trumpeting call. However, as recorded in a January 1986 report by the Soviet news agency *Tass* and later in Western newspapers, after studying the findings of the expeditions a team from the Soviet Academy of Sciences declared that these sounds were merely noises produced by air being sucked into cracks connecting the deep lake with underwater cavities, and

Eyewitnesses describe Turkey's Lake Ercek monster as a white aquatic horse.

in which large whirlpools appear that explain reports of turbulence in the lake, hitherto attributed to monsters. Notwithstanding this official explanation, sightings of the monster have continued to the present day.

Moving further west, one of the most unlikely homes for a water monster is Lake Zeegrzynski, eighteen miles north of Poland's capital, Warsaw, because this is an artificial (and hence very recent) lake. Nevertheless, in 1982 a bather in the lake was startled by a huge, slimy black head bearing what seemed to him to be rabbit-like ears, which suddenly surfaced near him. In a survey of lake monsters from continental Europe (*Fortean Times*, spring 1986), German researcher Ulrich Magin suggested that those "ears" could have been the barbels of a giant catfish, and the monster's estimated length of twenty feet an exaggeration. This identity allies it with comparable mystery beasts reported from as far afield as Africa's Lake Victoria and Upper Nile swamps, South America's Paraguayan Chaco, and Germany's Lake Zwischenahn.

Northward into Scandinavia leads to Sweden and the home of the famous Lake Storsjön monster. Less familiar are those monsters allegedly inhabiting Iceland's Lake Kleifarvatn, sited twenty miles south of Reykjavik. In November 1984, bird hunters Olafur Olafsson and Julius Asgeirsson saw what they assumed to be two rocks lying on the lake's shore. When they drew nearer, however, the "rocks" moved, revealing themselves to be a pair

When a Tooth Is Not the Truth

The evolution of humans and other primates is a particularly fruitful source of slip-ups in zoological systematics.

In 1922, for example, an intriguing fossil hominid skull was unearthed in Patagonia by scientist Dr. J. G. Wolf. It was estimated to be at least one million years old, thereby stirring up considerable anthropological interest and excitement. Until its discovery, the oldest hominid remains had been those of Java Man *Homo* (*Pithecanthropus*) *erectus javanicus*, dating back only 500,000 years.

Consequently, Dr. Wolf's most significant fossil was submitted with all speed to a committee of scientists in Buenos Aires for detailed examination, after which the skull's preeminence rapidly dissolved into acute embarrassment. As reported in London's *Evening News* on January 2, 1923, the committee's investigation revealed that the "skull" was nothing more than a curiously shaped stone.

Another of our ancestors bit the dust a few years later. It has been suggested frequently that hominoids inhabited North America at an appreciably earlier date than any of the estimates of several thousand years ago that are officially countenanced by science. Indeed, during the early 1920s it appeared that the existence of one such form was substantiated by solid existence in the shape of a fossil tooth. The tooth, obtained in Agate, Nebraska, was identified as that of a higher primate hitherto unknown to science, and dated back to the Pliocene epoch (seven to two million years ago). In an *American Museum Novitates* paper of April 25, 1922, Professor Henry Fairfield Osborn formally christened this new species *Hesperopithecus haroldcookii*.

Sadly, however, the fate of *Hesperopithecus* was soon transformed into as notable a wreck as that of its maritime namesake. Upon detailed reexamination of the tooth in question, Dr. William Gregory reported in *Science* on December 16, 1927, that it was derived from a fossil peccary, a close relation of the pig family.

A similar scenario took place just over twenty years later with one of Australia's most famous fossils. In 1870, zoologist Gerard Krefft had documented a fragment of a supposed human molar that had been found in New South Wales' Wellington Caves. It was embedded in deposits subsequently estimated to be 7,000 to 12,000 years old, together with the remains of extinct giant wombat-like creatures called *Diprotodon* and the equally deceased marsupial lion *Thylacoleo*. Ever since then, this tooth had been renowned in scientific circles as one of the most prominent items of anatomical evidence in support of the antiquity of humans in Australia.

The peccary—*Hesperopithecus* was one of its ancestors, not one of ours.

When closely examined in 1948 by Professor H. H. Finlayson of the South Australian Museum, however, it was swiftly unmasked by him in the journal *Nature* as nothing more significant than the posterior half of the upper fourth premolar from the right-hand jaw of *Protemnodon anak*—a giant Pleistocene wallaby.

A mixed parentage indeed for humanity. Whatever would Charles Darwin think?

Six-Legged Squids and Other Mollusk Mimics

Taxonomic tribulations are not exclusive to our own family tree either. Zoologists were naturally excited when they learned from Chilean natives of an apparently undescribed form of squid, which they called *polpo*, and from which they extracted a type of black ink, for according to these people, the creature only possessed six limbs. All known squids have eight normal tentacles, and an extra-long pair used for capturing prey.

Assuming this polpo to be a radically new squid species, it was dubbed *Sepia hexapus*. Sadly, its scientific significance was short-lived, because an examination of some polpo specimens revealed it to be a species of stick insect.

Childress, David H. "Living Pterodactyls." *World Explorer*, no. 4 (1994): 36–51.

Chorvinsky, Mark. "Creature On Ice." *Strange Magazine*, no. 15 (spring 1995): 17.

Clark, Jerome and Loren Coleman. *Creatures of the Outer Edge*. Warner: New York, 1970.

Clark, Leonard. *The Rivers Ran East*. Hutchinson: London, 1954.

Cohen, Daniel. *The Encyclopedia of Monsters*. Dodd, Mead: New York, 1982.

Coleman, Loren. *Mysterious America*. Faber & Faber: Winchester, 1983.

———. "The Menehune: Little People of the Pacific." *FATE*, vol. 42 (July 1989): 78–89.

Connor, Steve. "Lost Worlds Rich in Unique Wildlife [Vu Quang]." *The Independent on Sunday* (London, July 3, 1994).

Cook, Claire. "Seeing Fins [sawtooth river dolphin]." *BBC Wildlife*, vol. 13 (April 1995): 11.

Coppé, Philippe. "Une Population de Varans Géants Découverte en Papouasie." *Nord-Eclair & Nord-Natin* (France, December 27, 1978).

Davies, David M. *Journey Into the Stone Age*. Robert Hale: London, 1969.

Day, David. *The Doomsday Book of Animals*. Ebury: London, 1981.

de Freycinet, Louis, ed. *Voyage Autour du Monde…, Zoologie (Vol. 1)*. Pillet Aîné: Paris, 1824.

de Mulzon, Christian. "Walrus-Like Feeding Adaptation in a New Cetacean from the Pliocene of Peru." *Nature*, vol. 365 (October 21, 1993): 745–8.

de Prorok, Byron. *Dead Men Do Tell Tales*. George Harrap: London, 1943.

Dineson, Lars, et al. "A New Species and Genus of Terdicine Bird (Phasianidae, Terdicinae) from Tanzania: A Relict Form with Indo-Malayan Affinities." *Ibis*, vol. 136 (January 1994): 2–11.

Dinsdale, Tim. *The Leviathans*. Routledge & Kegan Paul: London, 1966. Rev. ed. Futura: London, 1976.

Domenech, Emanuel. *Missionary Adventures in Texas and Mexico: A Personal Narrative of Six Years' Sojourn in Those Regions*. Longman, Brown, Green, Longmans, and Roberts: London, 1858.

Dougan, Michael. "The Tahoe Monster and Other Legends of the Lake." *Image* (June 12, 1988): 2–6 .

Eberhart, George M. *Monsters: A Guide to Information on Unaccounted-for Creatures*. Garland: New York, 1983.

"EHA" [Aitken, E. A.]. *The Tribes on My Frontier: An Indian Naturalist's Foreign Policy*. W. Thacker: London, 1898.

Ellis, Richard. *Monsters of the Sea*. Alfred A. Knopf: New York, 1994.

Evans, Hilary, Karl P. N. Shuker, et al., consultants. *Almanac of the Uncanny*. Reader's Digest: Surry Hills, 1995.

Finlayson, H. H. "Antiquity of Man in Australia." *Nature*, vol. 162 (1948): 256.

Fitzsimons, F. W. *Snakes*. Hutchinson: London, 1932.

Flannery, Tim, et al. "A New Tree Kangaroo from Irian Jaya, Indonesia…." *Mammalia*, vol. 59 (1995): 65–84.

Furness, Robert W. "Predation on Ground-Nesting Seabirds by Island Populations of Red Deer *Cervus elaphus* and Sheep *Ovis*." *Journal of Zoology*, vol. 216 (March 1988): 565–73.

Glidden, George. "Frog-Like Monsters Attack Scientists." *Examiner* (place of publication in U.S.A. unknown, August 11, 1987).

Goodwin, George G. "Inopinatus—The Unexpected." *Natural History*, vol. 55 (November 1946): 404–6.

Gordon-Cumming, Constance F. *At Home in Fiji*. W. Blackwood: London, 1882.

Goss, Michael. "In Search of Giant Lizards." *The Unknown*, no. 6, (December 1985): 34–9.

———. "Do Giant Prehistoric Sharks Survive?" *FATE*, vol. 40 (November 1987): 32–41.

———. "The Sea-Serpent With Frills Attached." *The Unknown*, no. 29 (November 1987): 36-41.

Gosse, Philip H. *The Romance of Natural History*. James Nisbet: London, 1860.

Gray, J. E. "Habits of the 'Kakapo' and 'Macro' of New Zealand." *Annals and Magazine of Natural History*, vol. 18 (1846): 427.

Green, Lawrence. *Secret Africa*. Stanley Paul: London, 1936.

Greenwell, J. Richard, ed. "Evidence For New Bear Species in Nepal." *ISC Newsletter*, vol. 3 (spring 1984): 1–3.

———, ed. "New Nepal Bear Now in Doubt." *ISC Newsletter*, vol. 4 (spring 1985): 4.

———, ed. "On the Beach [Lake Kleifarvatn monsters]." *ISC Newsletter*, vol. 4 (autumn 1985): 10.

———, ed. "Stafford Lake Monster Caught." *ISC Newsletter*, vol. 4 (winter 1985): 8.

———, ed. "Who's *Your* Insurance Company?" *ISC Newsletter*, vol. 5 (spring 1986): 9–10.

———, ed. "Hippoturtleox." *ISC Newsletter*, vol. 5 (spring 1986): 10.

———, ed. "Giant Fish Reported in China." *ISC Newsletter*, vol. 5 (autumn 1986): 7–8.

———, ed. "Memphré Christened, Given Dual Citizenship." *ISC Newsletter*, vol. 6 (summer 1987): 7–8.

———, ed. "Giant Bear [*Irkuiem*] Sought by Soviets." *ISC Newsletter*, vol. 6 (winter 1987): 6–7.

Gregory, William K. "Hesperopithecus Apparently Not an Ape Nor a Man." *Science*, vol. 66 (December 16, 1927): 579–81.

Stay in Touch. . .

Llewellyn publishes hundreds of books on your favorite subjects.

On the following pages you will find listed some books now available on related subjects. Your local bookstore stocks most of these and will stock new Llewellyn titles as they become available. We urge your patronage.

Order by Phone

Call toll-free within the U.S. and Canada, 1–800–THE MOON.

In Minnesota call (612) 291–1970.

We accept Visa, MasterCard, and American Express.

Order by Mail

Send the full price of your order (MN residents add 7% sales tax) in U.S. funds to :

> Llewellyn Worldwide
> P. O. Box 64383, Dept. K673-4
> St. Paul, MN 55164–0383, U.S.A.

Postage and Handling

- $4.00 for orders $15.00 and under
- $5.00 for orders over $15.00
- No charge for orders over $100.00

We ship UPS in the continental United States. We cannot ship to P.O. boxes. Orders shipped to Alaska, Hawaii, Canada, Mexico, and Puerto Rico will be sent first-class mail.

International orders: Airmail—add freight equal to price of each book to the total price of order, plus $5.00 for each non-book item (audiotapes, etc.).

Surface mail: Add $1.00 per item

Allow 4–6 weeks delivery on all orders. Postage and handling rates subject to change.

Group Discounts

We offer a 20% quantity discount to group leaders or agents. You must order a minimum of 5 copies of the same book to get our special quantity price.

Free Catalog

Get a free copy of our color catalog *New Worlds of Mind and Spirit*. Subscribe for just $10.00 in the United States and Canada ($20.00 overseas, first class mail). Many bookstores carry *New Worlds*—ask for it!

Psychic Pets & Spirit Animals
True Stories from the Files of *FATE Magazine*

FATE Magazine Editorial Staff

In spite of all our scientific knowledge about animals, important questions remain about the nature of animal intelligence. Now, a large body of personal testimony compels us to raise still deeper questions. Are some animals, like some people, psychic? If human beings survive death, do animals? Do bonds exist between people and animals that are beyond our ability to comprehend?

Psychic Pets & Spirit Animals is a varied collection from the past 50 years of the real-life experiences of ordinary people with creatures great and small. You will encounter psychic pets, ghost animals, animal omens, extraordinary human-animal bonds, pet survival after death, phantom protectors and the weird creatures of cryptozoology. Dogs, cats, birds, horses, wolves, grizzly bears—even insects—are the heroes of shockingly true reports that illustrate just how little we know about the animals we think we know best.

The true stories in *Psychic Pets & Spirit Animals* suggest that animals are, in many ways, more like us than we think—and that they, too, can step into the strange and unknowable realm of the paranormal, where all things are possible.

1-56718-299-2, 272 pp., mass market, softcover **$4.99**

Strange Encounters
UFOs, Aliens & Monsters Among Us

Curt Sutherly

UFOs and ghost lights ... sky quakes and strange disappearances ... phantom creatures and cryptozoological oddities ... all of these mysterious phenomena make us acutely aware of how little we really understand our world and the universe beyond. *Strange Encounters* was written by an experienced journalist and ufologist who has interviewed and personally investigated many of the remarkable, yet true, events he documents in this collection.

Take a weird journey into the unexplained with 15 gripping stories gathered from the author's own journalistic investigations. From alien encounters to eyewitness disappearances to the Mars probe failure, these are puzzles without real solutions. But Curt Sutherly points out significant parallels between sightings in different parts of the United States, which add up to a pattern of strange occurrences—based on reliable sources—that cannot be intelligently dismissed. If you want the truth about these mysterious sightings and who's attempting to cover them up, then this book will wholly engross you.

1-56718-699-8, 272 pp., mass market, $5.99

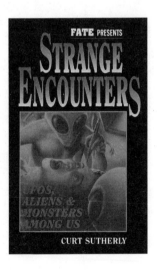

To order call 1–800–THE MOON

Prices subject to change without notice

True Hauntings
Spirits with a Purpose

Hazel M. Denning, Ph.D.

Do spirits feel and think? Does death automatically promote them to a paradise—or as some believe, a hell? Real-life ghostbuster Dr. Hazel M. Denning reveals the answers through case histories of the friendly and hostile earthbound spirits she has encountered. Learn the reasons spirits remain entrapped in the vibrational force field of the earth: fear of going to the other side, desire to protect surviving loved ones, and revenge. Dr. Denning also shares fascinating case histories involving spirit possession, psychic attack, mediumship and spirit guides. Find out why spirits haunt us in *True Hauntings*, the only book of its kind written from the perspective of the spirits themselves.

1-56718-218-6, 240 pp., 6 x 9, index, glossary, softcover   **$12.95**

To order call 1–800–THE MOON

Prices subject to change without notice